In Sync 1

Rod Fricker
Ingrid Freebairn
Jonathan Bygrave
Judy Copage

Welcome to the **Language Builder!**

This **Language Builder** will give you more practice in the grammar, vocabulary, functions, and skills that are in your Student Book. The Language Builder is divided into two parts: a Workbook and a Grammar Bank.

Workbook

The first part of the Language Builder is the **Workbook**. This contains practice exercises for the grammar, vocabulary, functions, and skills in your Student Book. Most of the exercises in the Workbook lessons are at two levels of difficulty: easier (★) and more difficult (★★). There are also *Consolidation* exercises, which provide practice of several language points. In addition, there is an *Extra challenge!* exercise (★★★) in each unit, which gives you the opportunity to do a more challenging activity.

Grammar Bank

The second part of the Language Builder is the **Grammar Bank**. This contains *Grammar Summary* pages with examples and notes to help you remember grammar rules. These are followed by *Grammar Practice* exercises. You can do these exercises as a follow-up to the exercises in the Workbook, or you can use them later to help you review.

We hope that this Language Builder will help you in your English studies.

Have fun and stay *In Sync*!

Contents

Workbook				Grammar Bank
Unit	Page	Grammar	Vocabulary/Function	Grammar
1A	2	• The verb *be*: singular • Subject pronouns and possessive adjectives	• Numbers 1–100	Page 99 • The verb *be*: singular • The verb *be*: plural • Subject pronouns and possessive adjectives
1B	4		• The alphabet • Days of the week • **Function:** Give personal information Greet people and say good-bye	
1C	6	• The verb *be*: plural • Subject pronouns	• Countries and nationalities	
1D	8	**Curriculum link:** Geography – *Far from home* **Integrated skills:** Consolidation **Learning strategy:** Scan for information		
2A	10	• Indefinite article: *a/an* • Regular nouns: plural • *This, that, these, those*	• Common objects	Page 102 • Indefinite article: *a/an* • Regular nouns: plural • *This, that, these, those* • Possessive *'s/s'* • Subject pronouns and possessive adjectives • *How much is . . ./How much are . . .*
2B	12	• Possessive *'s* (singular) and *s'* (plural) • Possessive adjectives: *our, your, their*	• Colors	
2C	14		• Fast food • Money • **Function:** Order food and drinks	
2D	16	**Values for living:** *Tim's birthday* **Integrated skills:** Consolidation **Learning strategy:** Listen a second time		
3A	18	• *There is/There isn't* or *There's no*, and *yes/no* questions • Definite article: *the*	• Rooms, parts of a house, fixtures, and appliances	Page 105 • *There is/There are* • *There isn't/There aren't* • Definite article: *the* • *Some/any* • Prepositions of place
3B	20	• *There are/There aren't*, and *yes/no* questions • *some* and *any* with plural nouns	• Furniture	
3C	22	• Prepositions of place: *in, on, under, behind, in front of, next to*	• **Function:** Make and respond to requests	
3D	24	**Across cultures:** *Houses* **Integrated skills:** Consolidation **Writing tip:** Punctuation		
4A	26	• *Have* with *I, you, we, they*	• Family • **Function:** Talk about your family	Page 108 • *Have* with *I, you, we, they* • *Has* with *he, she, it* • Prepositions of time: *in, on*
4B	28	• *Has* with *he, she, it*	• Appearance	
4C	30	• Prepositions of time: *in, on*	• Months and ordinal numbers • Seasons	
4D	32	**Curriculum link:** Science – *The Johansson twins* **Integrated skills:** Consolidation **Learning strategy:** Guess the meaning of new words		
5A	34	• Simple present with *I, you, we, they*	• Occupations	Page 111 • Simple present with *I, you, we, they* • Simple present with *he, she, it* • Object pronouns: *me, you, him, her, it, us, them*
5B	36	• Simple present with *he, she, it*	• Places of work	
5C	38	• Object pronouns: *me, you, him, her, it, us, them*	• Adjectives of opinion • **Function:** Exchange opinions	
5D	40	**Values for living:** *Problems at work* **Integrated skills:** Consolidation **Learning strategy:** Predict from the task		
6A	42	• Simple present with fixed times • Preposition of time: *at*	• Clock times	Page 115 • Simple present with fixed times • Adverbs of frequency • Adverbial expressions of frequency • Asking about frequency
6B	44	• Adverbs of frequency	• Daily routines	
6C	46	• Adverbial expressions of frequency	• **Function:** Express surprise and comment	
6D	48	**Across cultures:** *School days* **Integrated skills:** Consolidation **Writing tip:** *and, but, because, so*		

Contents

		Workbook		**Grammar Bank**
Unit	Page	Grammar	Vocabulary/Function	Grammar
7A	50	• Adverb: *(not) very well* • *Can* (present ability)	• Verbs of ability	Page 119 • *Can* (present ability)/ Adverb *(not) very well* • Count and noncount nouns with *some* and *any* • Imperatives • Prepositions of place
7B	52	• Count and noncount nouns with *some* and *any*	• Food	
7C	54	• Imperatives • Prepositions of place	• Places in town • **Function:** Ask for help in town	
7D	56	**Curriculum link:** Biology – *Healthy or unhealthy diet?* **Integrated skills:** Consolidation **Learning strategy:** Focus your reading		
8A	58	• Present continuous	• The weather	Page 123 • Present continuous • Simple present and present continuous • *Like, love, hate, prefer + -ing*
8B	60	• Simple present and present continuous	• Sports	
8C	62	• *Like, love, hate, prefer + -ing*	• Free-time activities • **Function:** Make and respond to suggestions	
8D	64	**Values for living:** *School blog* **Integrated skills:** Consolidation **Learning strategy:** Use pictures to predict		
9A	66	• Simple past of *be*	• Past adverbial expressions	Page 127 • Simple past of *be* • Simple past of regular verbs • Prepositions of motion
9B	68	• Simple past of regular verbs: affirmative and negative • Prepositions of motion		
9C	70	• Simple past of regular verbs: questions and short answers	• Adjectives of feeling • **Function:** Ask about problems	
9D	72	**Across cultures:** *Phones and flights* **Integrated skills:** Consolidation **Learning strategy:** Review your work		
10A	74	• Simple past of irregular verbs: affirmative and negative • *By* + means of transportation	• Transportation	Page 131 • Simple past of irregular verbs • *By* + means of transportation • Simple past with *ago*
10B	76	• Simple past of irregular verbs: questions	• Vacation activities • **Function:** Talk about vacations	
10C	78	• Simple past with *ago*	• Landforms	
10D	80	**Curriculum link:** History – *A new kind of explorer* **Integrated skills:** Consolidation **Learning strategy:** Skim to get the general idea		
11A	82	• Comparative and superlative of short adjectives	• Short adjectives	Page 135 • Comparative and superlative of short and long adjectives • *Which* + indefinite pronouns: *one/ones*
11B	84	• Comparative and superlative of long adjectives	• Adjectives of quality	
11C	86	• *Which* + indefinite pronoun: *one/ones*	• Clothes • **Function:** Shopping for clothes	
11D	88	**Values for living:** *Making friends* **Integrated skills:** Consolidation **Learning strategy:** Listen for general meaning		
12A	90	• *Be* + *going to* for future plans and intentions	• Types of music	Page 139 • *Be* + *going to* for future plans and intentions • Possessive pronouns • Question word: *Whose . . . ?* • *Want* + infinitive • *Want* + object pronoun + infinitive
12B	92	• Possessive pronouns • Question word: *Whose . . . ?*	• Adverbs	
12C	94	• *Want* + infinitive • *Want* + object pronoun + infinitive	• **Function:** Invite, accept, and refuse	
12D	96	**Across cultures:** *Music festivals* **Integrated skills:** Consolidation **Writing tip:** Organize your ideas		

Hello

1

Phrases

1 ★ Complete the three conversations with the correct phrases from the box.

> • How are you? • Nice to meet you.
> • Thanks. • This is

A: Hello, Tom. **1** _How are you?_

B: Fine, thanks, Steve. And you?

A: Oh, Dan. **2** _____ Kelly.

B: Hi, Kelly. **3** _____

A: What's that?

B: It's my new cell phone.

A: It's cool.

B: **4** _____

Vocabulary: Numbers 1–100

2 ★ Write out the numbers.

80	15	12
1 _eighty_	2 f_____	3 t_____
20	13	41
4 t_____	5 t_____	6 f_____
92	100	
7 n_____	8 o___h_____	

Grammar: The verb _be_: singular

3 ★ Circle the correct choice.

1 A: Hello. Who _am / is / are_ you?

2 B: Hi. I _'m / 's / 're_ Leo. What's your name?

3 A: My name _'m / 's / 're_ Carla.

4 B: _Am / Is / Are_ you 15, Carla?

5 A: Yes, I _'m / am / is_. That's a cool phone.

6 B: Thanks. _He's / She's / It's_ from Japan.

4 ★★ Complete the questions and answers. Use the correct form of _be_.

A: **1** _Is_ your name Max?

B: No, it **2** _____ .

A: What **3** _____ your name?

B: My name's Ethan.

A: **4** _____ _____ American?

B: Yes, I **5** _____ .

A: What's that?

B: **6** _____ my cell phone.

A: **7** _____ Sara your sister?

B: No, **8** _____ _____ .

A: How old **9** _____ you?

B: **10** _____ 16.

Grammar: Subject pronouns and possessive adjectives

5 ★ Complete the chart.

Subject pronouns	Possessive adjectives
I	**1** *my*
you	**2**
3	his
she	**4**
it	**5**

6 ★★ Complete the three conversations with subject pronouns or possessive adjectives.

Anna: Hi. What's **1** *your* name?

Kevin: 2 _____ name's Kevin.

Anna: Nice to meet **3** _____ , Kevin.

    4 _____ name's Anna. Is she

    5 _____ sister?

Kevin: Yes, **6** _____ is. **7** _____

    name's Emma.

Kay: What's that?

Tom: 8 _____ 's my cell phone.

Kay: 9 _____ ring tone is cool.

Lucy: Who's he?

Sara: 10 _____ name's

    Barry Blue.

    11 _____ 's cool.

Consolidation

7 Complete the conversation with the phrases (a–h) from the box.

> a) No, I'm the youth coordinator.
> b) She's Jenny.
> c) Hi, Phil. How are things?
> d) Nice to meet you, Phil.
> e) I'm OK.
> f) How old are you, Chris?
> g) Sixteen. Hey, Jenny. Hi!
> h) It's my new cell phone.

Phil: Hello, Chris.

Chris: 1 *Hi, Phil. How are things?* _____

Phil: Fine, thanks. How are you?

Chris: 2 _____

Phil: What's that?

Chris: 3 _____

Phil: Cool. Hey, who's she?

Chris: 4 _____

Phil: How old is she?

Chris: 5 _____

Jenny: Hi, Chris.

Chris: Jenny, this is Phil. Phil, this is Jenny.

Jenny: 6 _____

Phil: And you.

Jenny: 7 _____

Chris: I'm 15. Is this your first time here?

Jenny: 8 _____

Chris: Oh . . .

3

1B What's your address?

Function: Give personal information

1 ★ Read and answer the questions.

This is Julia Moran. She's 15 years old. Her address is 41 Brook Street, Seattle, WA. The zip code is 98104. Her home phone number is (206) 555-1796. Today, she's at the Seattle Youth Club to register.

A: Hello. I'm here to register.
B: Oh, yes. Hi. What's your first name?
A: **1** *Julia.*
B: OK, and what's your last name?
A: **2** _____
B: Sorry. How do you spell that?
A: **3** _____
B: Thank you. Now, how old are you?
A: **4** _____
B: What's your address, including zip code?
A: **5** _____
_____
B: What's your home phone number?
A: **6** _____
B: Thank you very much. Here's your card.

Vocabulary: The alphabet

2 ★ Circle the letter with a different sound.

1 A J (G) K   4 F L M H
2 B D E S   5 C S X L
3 Q Y W U   6 C J G T

Vocabulary: Days of the week

3 ★ Answer these questions.

QUIZ ? ? ? ?

1 Today is Monday. What day is tomorrow?
Tuesday

2 Today and tomorrow are the weekend. What day is today?
_____

3 Today is Sunday. What day is tomorrow?
_____

4 Tomorrow is Saturday. What day is today?
_____

5 Today is Tuesday. What day is tomorrow?
_____

6 Tomorrow is Friday. What day is today?
_____

7 Today is the weekend. Tomorrow isn't the weekend. What day is today?
_____

8 Tomorrow is Wednesday. What day is it today?
_____

Use your English:
Greet people and say good-bye

4 ★ Complete the chart by writing the number of the phrase (1–8) in the correct column.

1 Hi!   5 Good night.
2 How are you?   6 Good morning.
3 Bye.   7 OK, thanks.
4 Fine, thanks. 8 How are things?

Say hello	Say good-bye	Ask about somebody	Respond
1			

5 ★★ Circle the correct words.

1 (Good morning) / Bye, Leo.

2 Hi / Good night, Mrs. Mitchell.

3 Who / How / What are you, Leo?

4 I'm Leo / fine / bad, thank you.

5 Good. Here's Jack. Hi / Good morning /
Good-bye, Leo. See you later, Jack.

6 Good morning / Good-bye / Hello, Mrs. Mitchell.

Consolidation

6 Match the questions (1–10) to the correct responses (a–j).

1 ~~What's your first name?~~	d
2 What's your last name?	
3 What's your address?	
4 What's your zip code?	
5 What's your phone number?	
6 What day is it today?	
7 How do you spell your last name?	
8 Is that your home phone number?	
9 How are you?	
10 How old are you?	

a) It's Saturday.
b) It's 31 Spring Street, Seattle, WA.
c) I'm fine, thanks.
d) ~~John.~~
e) I'm 14.
f) It's 98101.
g) No, it isn't. It's my cell number.
h) It's Smith.
i) (206) 555-0134
j) S–M–I–T–H.

Extra challenge!

7 ★★★ Look at the answers and write the questions.

Shelton YOUTH CLUB

6 Laurel Street, Shelton, WA 98584

August 10th

Dear Miss King,

Here is your registration card.

Shelton YOUTH CLUB

REGISTRATION CARD

Alice King
146 Holly Lane,
Shelton, WA 98584
Tel: (360) 555-4698
Age: 15

1 _What's her first name?_____
Alice.

2 _____
King.

3 _____
146 Holly Lane, Shelton, WA.

4 _____
98584.

5 _____
(360) 555-4698.

6 _____
Fifteen.

Where are you from?

Vocabulary: Countries

1 ★ Look at the maps. Then write the name of the country below.

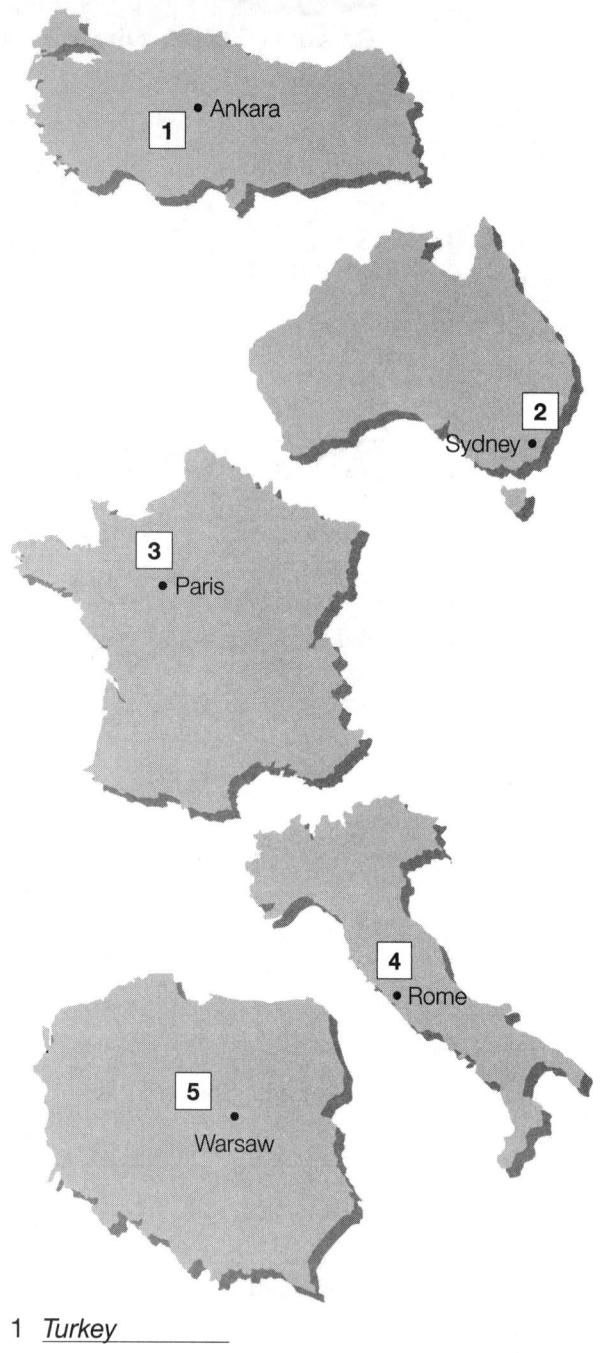

1 *Turkey* _____

2 _____

3 _____

4 _____

5 _____

Vocabulary: Countries and nationalities

2 ★ Complete the chart.

Country	Nationality
1 *the U.K.*	British
2 Argentina	
3	Brazilian
4 Canada	
5	French
6 Mexico	
7	Italian
8 the U.S.	
9	Portuguese
10 Russia	

3 ★★ Circle the correct words.

1 Paolo's
Italy / (*Italian*).

2 Marianna's from
Greece / Greek.

3 Marie's from
France / French.

4 Boris is
Russia / Russian.

5 José's *Portugal /*
Portuguese.

6 Kazuko's
Japan / Japanese.

Grammar: The verb *be*: plural

4 ★ Complete the sentences with the correct plural subject pronoun.

1 Jack, Chris, and I are 16. *We*'re 16.

2 Dean and Renée are 15. _____'re 15.

3 You and Renée are French. _____'re French.

4 Inez and I are Spanish. _____'re Spanish.

5 Dean and Jack are British. _____'re British.

6 You and Inez are 16. _____'re 16.

5 ★ Complete the questions and answers.

1 A: Marco and Inez / where / you from?

Marco and Inez, where are you from?

B: (from Spain)

We're from Spain.

2 A: where / Dean and Jack from?

_____

B: (from the U.K.)

_____

3 A: Dean and Jack / American?

_____

B: (No)

_____

4 A: Jack and Dean / you / 17?

_____

B: (No, 15)

_____

5 A: how old / Renée and Dean?

_____

B: (15)

_____

6 A: Renée and Claude / you / French?

_____

_____

B: (Yes)

_____

7 A: how old / you and Jack?

_____

B: (16)

_____

6 ★★ Complete the sentences with the correct choices from the box.

> • are • are • are • aren't • He • It • It • 're
> • 's • They • We

Hi! My name's Peter. This is my girlfriend, Molly. **1** We *'re* 16. **2** _____'re from Boulder. Boulder is a nice city. **3** _____'s in Colorado in the U.S. My parents **4** _____ teachers in Boulder.

This is Felipe and his sister Maria. Felipe **5** _____ 17. **6** _____'s a singer. Maria's seven. **7** _____'re Brazilian. Felipe and Maria **8** _____ from Recife. **9** _____'s a very big city. Boulder and Recife **10** _____ big cities, but they **11** _____ capital cities.

Consolidation

7 Circle the correct words.

Ben: Hi. My name's Ben, and this is Denise.

Adam: Hello. I'm Adam, and this is Renata.

Ben: Where are **1** *we /*(*you*)*/ they* from, Adam?

Adam: **2** *It's / We're / They're* from Poland, from Bielsko. Are **3** *you / we / they* American?

Ben: I'm American, but Denise isn't. **4** *She's / We're / They're* from Perth, Australia.

Adam: Who **5** *they are / they / are they*?

Ben: They're Paula and Marianna.

Adam: Are **6** *they / we / you* American?

Ben: No, they **7** *not / isn't / aren't*. Paula is **8** *the U.K./ England / British*, and Marianna's from **9** *Brazilian / Chile / Chinese*.

Far from home

Cristiano Ronaldo

My name's Cristiano Ronaldo. I'm from Funchal. It's the capital of the islands of Madeira, but it isn't a big town. The islands are Portuguese. My full name is Cristiano Ronaldo dos Santos Aveiro. My first language is Portuguese. I'm a soccer player in Madrid, a big city in Spain. Now, I speak English. It's important for my job. I travel all over the world, and many people in other countries speak English.

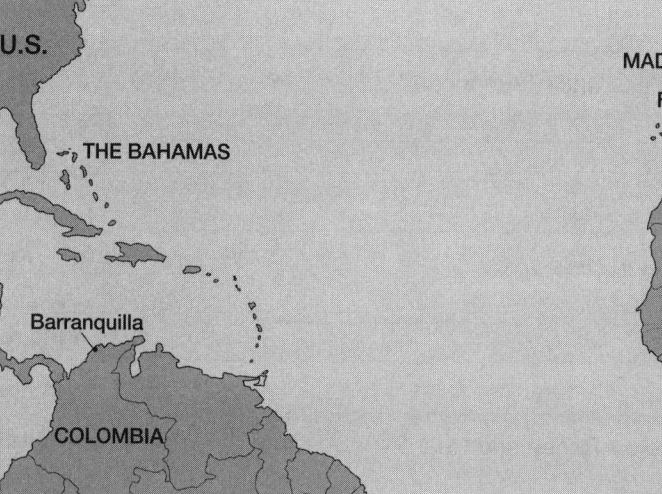

U.S.

MADEIRA

Funchal

THE BAHAMAS

Barranquilla

COLOMBIA

Shakira

My name's Shakira. I'm a singer. I'm from Barranquilla in Colombia. It's a big city. My full name is Shakira Isabel Mebarak Ripoll. I speak Spanish and English. English is important for my job. My songs are in English and Spanish. My home is now in the Bahamas, an English-speaking country. They are islands near the U.S.

Before you read

1 **Before you read, check the meaning of these words.**

New words
- soccer player • island • singer

Learning strategy: Scan for information

Remember! When you want to find specific information in a text, you **scan** it. When you scan, you don't need to read every word. For example, to find names, places, countries, nationalities, and languages in a text, look for words that begin with capital letters.

Read

2 ★ **Scan the article and find the answers to the questions. Write CR (Cristiano Ronaldo) or S (Shakira).**

1 I'm from an island.   *CR*

2 My home's on an island now.   _____

3 My hometown's a capital.   _____

4 I speak Spanish.   _____

5 My hometown's big.   _____

6 I speak Portuguese.   _____

7 My hometown isn't big.   _____

3 ★★ **Read the article again and correct the sentences.**

1 Cristiano Ronaldo's from Lisbon.

   He isn't from Lisbon. He's from Funchal.

2 Funchal is the capital of Portugal.

   _____

   _____

3 The islands of Madeira are Spanish.

   _____

   _____

4 Shakira's a soccer player.

   _____

   _____

5 Barranquilla is a small city.

   _____

   _____

6 Shakira's songs are in Spanish and French.

   _____

   _____

7 Shakira's home is in the U.S.

   _____

   _____

Listen

4 ★ 🎧 **2** **Listen. Where is the girl from?**

a) Canada   b) South Africa   c) Australia

5 ★★ 🎧 **2** **Listen again and complete the information.**

1 First name: _____

2 Last name: _____

3 From (country): _____

4 From (city): _____

5 Number of official languages: _____

6 Languages: _____ and _____

7 Reason English is important: _____

   _____

Write

6 ★ **Read the information card and write about Mai Lu in your notebook. Use the text about Santiago on page 11 of the Student Book to help you.**

Name: Mai Lu
From: Singapore City, Singapore
Speaks: English, Chinese
Official languages of Singapore: English, Chinese, Mandarin, Malay, Tamil
Reason English is important: Internet chat—friends in Australia and the U.S.

Your life

2

Vocabulary: Common objects

1 ★ Complete the words.

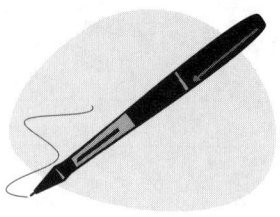

1 p _e_ n

2 a _pp_ l e

3 c _ _ _ _ _ a

4 b _ _ _ _

5 h _ _

6 I _ _ _ _ _ _

7 c _ _ _ _   p _ _ _ _ _

8 MP3 p _ _ _ _ _ _

Grammar: Indefinite article: *a/an*

2 ★ Complete the sentences with *a* or *an*.

1 It's _a_ pen.

2 It's _an_ apple.

3 It's ___ key.

4 It's ___ hat.

5 It's ___ address.

6 It's ___ ID card.

7 It's ___ notebook.

8 It's ___ sandwich.

Grammar: Regular nouns: plural

3 ★ Look. Complete the sentences.

1 They*'re books*.

2 They _____ .

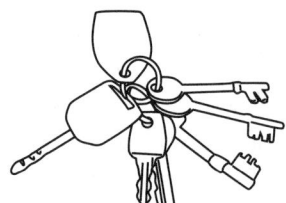

3 They _____ .

4 They _____ .

5 They _____ .

6 They _____ .

4 ★★ Correct the mistake in each sentence.

1 It's T-shirt. ✗

   It's a T-shirt.

2 They're my sandwichs. ✗

   _____

3 It isn't a apple. ✗

   _____

4 They's pens. ✗

   _____

5 It's an hat. ✗

   _____

Phrases

5 ★ Match the responses (a–d) to the correct statements or questions (1–4).

1 Where are my keys? **b**

2 My sandwiches and my sneakers are in this bag. ☐

3 Your ring tone is awful. ☐

4 Here's my homework. ☐

a) Don't be silly. It's cool.
b) ~~I don't know.~~
c) That's great!
d) Yuck! That's disgusting.

Grammar: *This, that, these, those*

6 ★ Complete the sentences with words from the box.

• that • these • ~~this~~ • those

1 *This* is my book.   2 _____ are your books.

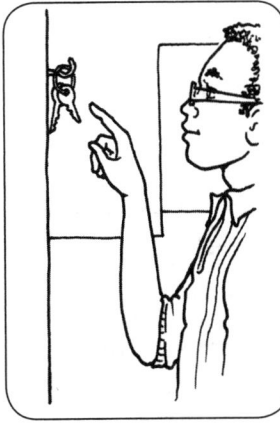 

3 _____ are my keys.   4 _____ is her key.

7 ★★ Ask and answer questions about the pictures.

 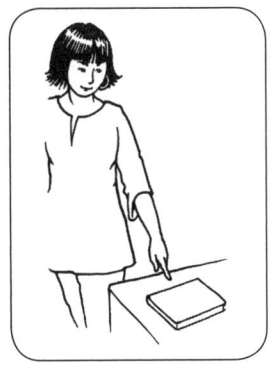

1 What *are these*?   2 What's _____ ?
   They're *notebooks*.   It's _____ .

3 What _____ ?   4 What's _____ ?
   They're _____ .   It's _____ .

Consolidation

8 Circle the correct choice.

1 A: What's (*this*)/ *these*?
   B: It's *a* / *an* camera.

2 A: What *is* / *are* these?
   B: *It's* / *They're* sneakers.

3 A: What *is this* / *that*?
   B: It's *a* / *an* key.

4 A: What *'s* / *'re* that?
   B: It's *a* / *an* ID card.

5 A: *Is* / *Are* this your hat?
   B: Yes, *it is* / *they are*.

6 A: Are these your *sandwich* / *sandwiches*?
   B: No. Yuck! *They're* / *It's* disgusting!

2B We're at Carla's house.

Grammar: Possessive 's (singular) and s' (plural)

1 ★ **Write S for singular possessive or P for plural possessive.**

1 This is my <u>friend's</u> dog.   _S_

2 These aren't my <u>teachers'</u> books.   _____

3 Is this your <u>brother's</u> ID card?   _____

4 Are these your <u>sister's</u> keys?   _____

2 ★★ **Put an apostrophe in the correct place.**

This is Sams ID card.

This is Sam's ID card.

Are these Annas sneakers?

_____

_____

Those aren't my

parents cars.

_____

_____

These are the boys T-shirts.

_____

_____

This is my teachers apple.

_____

These are two friends dogs.

_____

Grammar: Possessive adjectives: our, your, their

3 ★ **Read. Write the correct house number.**

Hello, Tom. This is Joe, and this is wrong! We're in your house, you're in their house, and they're in our house!

Joe and Mary

Tom and Kate

Steve and Betty

1 Joe and Mary's house is number _____ .

2 Tom and Kate's house is number _____ .

3 Steve and Betty's house is number _____ .

4 ★★ **Now complete what Tom says to Joe.**

Tom: Right! We're in 1 _____ house, you're in

2 _____ house, and they're in 3 _____ house!

12

5 ★★ Rewrite the sentences using a plural possessive adjective.

1 The dogs' names are Benji and Rufus.

Their names are Benji and Rufus.

2 Your sneakers are blue. My sneakers are blue.

Our sneakers are blue.

3 My friends' phones are cool.

_____

4 Kim, your keys are here. Su, your keys are here.

_____

5 My parents' names are Camilo and Maria.

_____

6 My T-shirt is white. My brother's T-shirt is white.

_____

Vocabulary: Colors

6 ★ Look at the picture. Label the objects with the correct color.

1 yellow
2 b_____
3 r_____
4 g_____
5 g_____
6 b_____
7 b_____
8 y_____

Consolidation

7 Circle the correct words.

Hi! My name's Mark, and this is my sister.

We live with 1 *our* / *their* parents in Fresno.

My 2 *sisters'* / *sister's* name is Allison.

My sister's best 3 *friends* / *friends'* are Rachel and Eve.

4 *Rachel's* / *Rachels'* brother, Scott, is my best friend.

Scott and I are in a band.

5 *Their* / *Our* band's name is "The Blue Guitars."

6 *Scott* / *Scott's* guitar is blue.

My 7 *parent's* / *parents'* favorite possessions

are 8 *our* / *their* cell phones.

My 9 *mom* / *mom's* phone is red, and my

10 *dad's* / *dads'* phone is black.

My favorite pets are my dogs.

11 *Our* / *Their* names are Rex and Fido.

12 *They're* / *Their* great!

How much is that?

Vocabulary: Fast food

1 ★ **Unscramble the letters and write the words.**

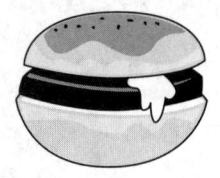

1 rugrbe

burger

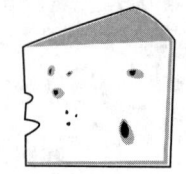

2 seehec

_____

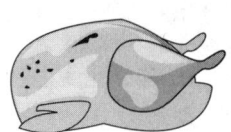

3 necickh

_____

4 aotpto scihp

_____

5 nageor cujei

_____

6 ate

_____

7 fofeec

_____

8 tobdtel trawe

_____

9 tho coolteach

_____

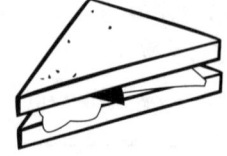

10 winchads

_____

Vocabulary: Money

2 ★ **Match the prices (1–8) to the correct words (a–h).**

1 25¢   a) Five dollars and sixty cents

2 70¢   b) Fifteen dollars

3 $1.40   c) Fifty-six cents

4 $5   d) Fifteen cents

5 $5.60   e) Twenty-five cents

6 15¢   f) Five dollars

7 $15   g) One dollar and forty cents

8 56¢   h) Seventy cents

3 ★★ **Write how much the food orders are altogether.**

Bottled water	99¢
Cheese sandwich	$3.50
Total:	$4.49

1 That's _four dollars and forty-nine cents_ altogether.

Hot chocolate	95¢
Potato chips	75¢
Total:	

2 That's _____ altogether.

Tea	80¢
Soda	$1.25
Total:	

3 That's _____ altogether.

Ice cream	$1.50
Ice cream	$1.50
Ice cream	$1.50
Total:	

4 That's _____ altogether.

Burger	$4.25
Coffee	$1.50
Total:	

5 That's _____ altogether.

Use your English: Order food and drinks

MENU

BURGERS	$3.25
SODA	95¢
HOT DOGS	$2.00
JUICE	
orange	99¢
SANDWICHES	
chicken	$3.50
cheese	$2.50
COFFEE	$1.25

4 ★ Number the conversation in the correct order.

Server

a) They're $3.25. ☐

b) Here you are. ☐

c) Good morning. ☐ 1

d) Orange juice is 99¢. ☐

e) That's $4.24. Thank you. Good-bye. ☐ 9

Customer

f) Thanks. How much is that altogether, please? ☐

g) And how much is the orange juice? ☐

h) OK, can I have a burger and orange juice, please? ☐

i) Good morning. How much are the burgers? ☐ 2

Consolidation

5 Write the words in the correct order to make conversations.

1 you / are. / Here

A: *Here you are.*

you. / Thank

B: *Thank you.*

2 sandwich, / I / a / Can / please? / have

A: _____

chicken? / Cheese / or

B: _____

3 please? / much / water, / is / How / bottled

A: _____

_____

cents. / It's / ninety-nine

B: _____

4 that / How / altogether? / is / much

A: _____

sixty cents. / dollars / four / and / That's

B: _____

5 else? / Anything

A: _____

of / coffee, / Yes, / a / please / cup.

B: _____

Extra challenge!

6 ★★★ Look at the menu and the conversation in Exercise 4. Write your own conversation.

Menu

Food	
Chicken sandwich	$3.50
Burger	$3.50
Hot dog	$2.50
Drinks	
Bottled water	75¢
Soda	$1.10
Coffee	$1.30
Tea	99¢

Values for living
Tim's birthday

1 ★ Skim the two conversations to find and check (✓) the things Tim gets for his birthday.

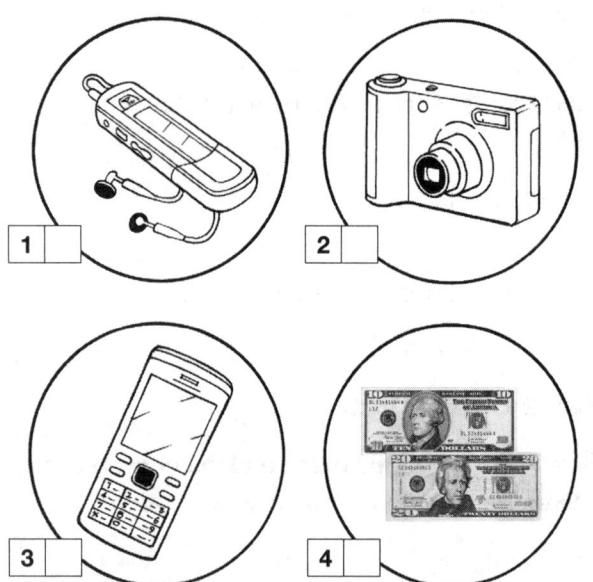

1 ☐ 2 ☐

3 ☐ 4 ☐

Mom: Hello, dear.

Dad: Hello.

Mom: 1 *What's that?*

Dad: It's an MP3 player.

Mom: For you?

Dad: No! It's a present.

Mom: For who?

Dad: For Tim! It's his birthday next week!

Mom: Oh right!

* * * * * * * * * * * *

Mom: 2 _____ Here's your present.

Tim: What is it? . . . Oh, wow! An MP3 player. Cool.

Mom: Do you like it?

Tim: Yes, it's great. The colors are cool.

3 _____ It's the same color as Jamie's. You're fantastic Mom.

4 _____ Thanks!

Mom: And here's some money from Mr. and Mrs. Davies.

Tim: Oh great . . . wow! $30. With my money, that's $80 altogether. Er . . . Mom, Dad, can I borrow some money from you?

Mom: What for?

Tim: For a camera.

Dad: 5 _____

Tim: About $152. Can I borrow $72?

Dad: $72? You're joking. That's your allowance for 12 weeks! No!

2 ★ Read the conversations again and put sentences (a–e) in the correct places (1–5).

a) Happy birthday, Tim.

b) Silver and black.

c) How much is it?

d) ~~What's that?~~

e) And so are you, Dad.

3 ★ Read the conversations again and circle the correct answers.

1 It's *Tim's* birthday next week.
  a) Tim's mother's
  b) Tim's father's
  c) Tim's

2 The MP3 player is for _____ .
  a) Tim
  b) Tim's mother
  c) Tim's father

3 Tim thinks the MP3 player is a(n) _____ present.
  a) awful
  b) very good
  c) disgusting

4 Jamie's MP3 player is _____ .
  a) expensive
  b) silver and black
  c) new

5 Tim asks his mother and father for _____ .
  a) $80
  b) $152
  c) $72

6 Tim's allowance is _____ a week.
  a) $12
  b) $6
  c) $30

Listen

Learning strategy: Listen a second time

Remember! When you listen for the first time, you won't understand everything. Don't worry! The next time you listen, you will understand more.

4 ★ 🎧 3 Listen and circle the correct amounts.

1 Jim's allowance is *$8 / $16* a week.

2 Jim's mom gives him *$8 / $16*.

3 The black T-shirt is *$8 / $16*.

4 A ticket for the band is *$8 / $16*.

5 ★★ 🎧 3 Listen again and circle the correct answers.

1 Jim's mom gives him his allowance. It is . . .
  a) $16. b) $8. c) $10.

2 He borrows the money from . . .
  a) his sister. b) his mother. c) his friend.

3 He wants to buy . . .
  a) a T-shirt. b) a book. c) sneakers.

4 The yellow T-shirt is . . .
  a) cool. b) awful. c) expensive.

5 The black T-shirt is . . .
  a) the same as the yellow T-shirt.
  b) awful.
  c) cool.

6 Jim's favorite color is …
  a) black. b) yellow. c) red.

Write

6 ★ Elena wants a new hat. Use the pictures and the words in the box to write a conversation in your notebook between Elena and her dad. Use conversation 3 on page 19 of the Student Book to help you.

> • hat • $36 • allowance
> • $4 a week • Dad / Elena

$36

YELLOW
COOL
EXPENSIVE

There's no bathtub.

Vocabulary: Rooms, parts of a house, fixtures, and appliances

1 ★ Look at the pictures and unscramble the letters to make words.

1 lawl

wall

2 argferiotrer

_____

3 gindni moro

_____

4 horbomat

_____

5 rewosh

_____

6 tenhick

_____

7 kins

_____

8 warsheshdi

_____

9 givnil moro

_____

10 rofol

_____

11 owdiwn

_____

12 rodo

_____

2 ★★ Write the fixture or appliance from the box by the correct room.

> • ~~bathtub~~ • dishwasher • refrigerator • shower
> • big sink • stove • small sink • toilet

• **Bathroom** *bathtub* _____ , _____ ,

_____ , _____

• **Kitchen** _____ , _____ ,

_____ , _____

Grammar: *There is/There isn't* or *There's no . . .*

3 ★ Look at the advertisement and write sentences with *there is* or *there isn't*.

> ## Student apartment for rent
>
> **Great appliances and much, much more!**
>
> • **Four rooms**
>   Kitchen (big)
>   Bedroom
>   Living room
>   Bathroom
>
> • **New:**
>   Stove
>   Refrigerator
>   Shower
>
> ★ Big window in the living room
>
> **Telephone: Mrs. Daley 617-555-1234**

1 (kitchen) *There's a kitchen.*

2 (dining room) _____

_____

3 (bathtub) _____

4 (garage) _____

5 (refrigerator) _____

6 (shower) _____

7 (living room) _____

_____

8 (dishwasher) _____

_____

9 (washing machine) _____

_____

4 ★★ Complete the conversation about the apartment in Exercise 3. Use the correct form of *there is*.

Natalie: Hello. Is this Mrs. Daley?

Mrs. Daley: Yes.

Natalie: Can you tell me about the student apartment?

Mrs. Daley: Yes, of course.

Natalie: **1** *Is there* a dining room?

Mrs. Daley: No, **2** _____ , but **3** _____ a big kitchen.

Natalie: OK. **4** _____ a washing machine?

Mrs. Daley: No, **5** _____ .

Natalie: OK. Can I come and see the apartment?

Mrs. Daley: Yes, of course.

Grammar: Definite article: *the*

5 ★ Circle the correct words.

Julio,

There's **1** (a) / an / the sandwich and
2 a / an / the apple for you in **3** a / an / the kitchen, and there's **4** a / an / the letter for your teacher in your bag. Don't forget it!

Buy **5** a / an / the pizza to eat in
6 a / an / the afternoon. There's some money in your bag. See you about eight.

Mom

PS There's **7** a / an / the notebook in
8 a / an / the garage and **9** a / an / the watch in **10** a / an / the bathroom. They're your things! Put them in your bag or your bedroom.

Consolidation

6 Write about each room. Use the correct form of *there is/are*.

1 There's *a living room* in my house.

(bag) *There's a bag in the living room.*

(fridge) *There isn't a refrigerator in the living room.*

(door?) *Is there a door in the living room?*
        Yes, there is.

2 There's _____ in my house.

(shower) _____

(bathtub?) _____

(small sink) _____

3 _____ in my house.

(washing machine?) _____

(stove) _____

(dishwasher) _____

4 _____ in my house.

(dresser?) _____

(window) _____

(sink) _____

Vocabulary: Furniture

1 ★ **Label the picture.**

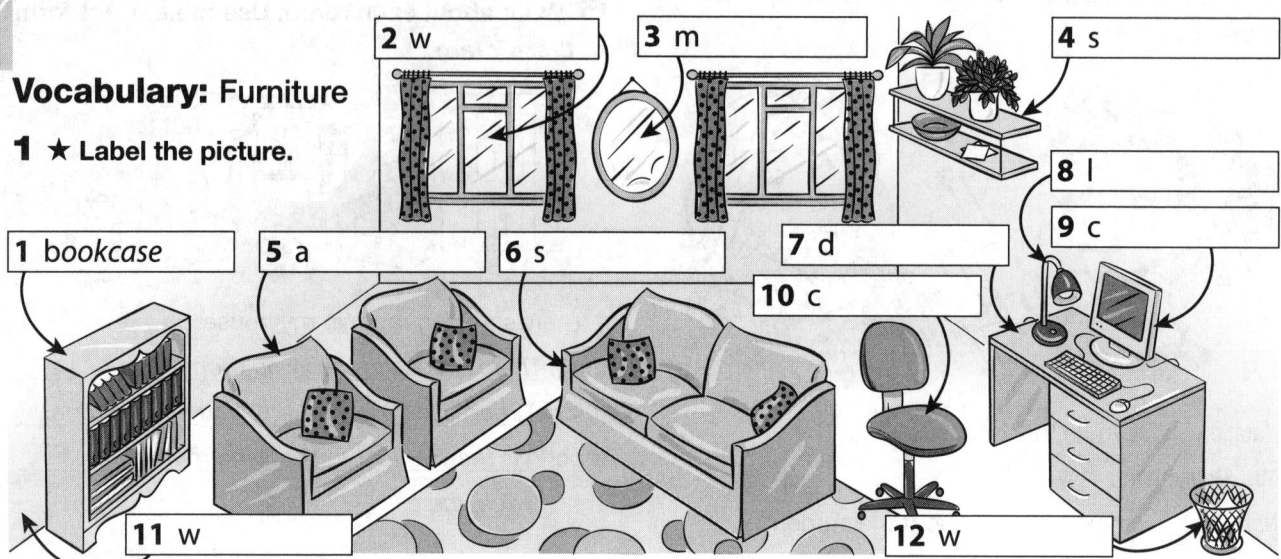

| 2 w | 3 m | 4 s |
| 1 bookcase | 5 a | 6 s | 7 d | 8 l | 9 c |
| 10 c |
| 11 w | 12 w |

Phrases

2 ★ **Circle the correct phrases.**

1 A: Hey, there are some of my old videos in here.

  B: *Let's see.* / *Sorry.*

2 A: Is there a computer in your house?

  B: Not yet. *Sorry.* / *Let's see.*

3 A: There's an old Rambo movie on TV today.

  B: *Sorry, not really my kind of movie.* / *I'm afraid.*

4 A: It's Friday night! No homework, burger and potato chips to eat, and a great DVD. *Sorry.* / *What do you think?*

  B: *Shrek 3*? It's not really my kind of movie!

Grammar: *There are/There aren't*

3 ★ **Look at the picture in Exercise 1. Match 1–8 with a–h to make true sentences.**

1 There's	a) a clock.
2 There are	b) TV.
3 There aren't	c) a dresser?
4 There isn't	d) a lamp.
5 Is there	e) any bookcases?
6 There's a	f) any CDs.
7 Are there	g) mirror.
8 There isn't a	h) some chairs.

4 ★★ **Complete the conservation with the correct form of *there is* or *there are*.**

A: Hi, Stacey. How's your new house?

B: It's OK. The living room's pretty big. **1** *There are* lots of bookcases.

A: What's your bedroom like?

B: It's big. **2** _____ two armchairs and **3** _____ some lamps.

A: **4** _____ a DVD player in your room?

B: No, **5** _____ .

A: **6** _____ a TV in your room?

B: No, **7** _____ . We can't afford it.

A: **8** _____ any cabinets?

B: No, **9** _____ , but **10** _____ a desk and a computer.

Grammar: *Some* and *any* with plural nouns

5 ★ **Circle the correct words.**

1 Are there *some* / *any* / *a* chairs in your room?

2 There *isn't* / *aren't* / *are* some DVDs.

3 There is *some* / *any* / *a* sofa.

4 There *isn't* / *aren't* / *are* any televisions.

5 Is there *some* / *any* / *a* computer?

6 There aren't *some* / *any* / *a* tables in the house.

6 ★★ Complete the letter with the correct form of *there are* (+ affirmative, – negative, or ? question) and *some* or *any*.

Dear Mario,

Thanks for your letter and the photos of your house. **1** (–) *There aren't any* houses like that here. **2** (+) _____ nice houses, but they aren't very big.

In our house, there are five rooms: a kitchen, a living room, a bathroom, and two bedrooms. My two brothers and I are in one bedroom. **3** (–) _____ cabinets or dressers in our room. **4** (–) _____ shelves, but **5** (+) _____ _____ nice bookcases. In your next letter, please tell me about your school. **6** (?) _____ computers in your classroom? **7** (?) _____ _____ students from other countries?

Bye for now,
Juan

Consolidation

7 Complete the conversation with words from the box.

> • afraid • any • ~~are~~ • are • aren't • dresser
> • Is • kind • player • see • some

Rebecca: Wow, there **1** <u>are</u> some great things here for the youth club. Look . . .

Tim: Oh yes. A sofa and two old armchairs.

Rebecca: **2** _____ there a desk?

Tim: No, there isn't, but there's a table.

Rebecca: There **3** _____ any wastebaskets, but I can borrow some from my mom. Are there **4** _____ lamps?

Tim: Yes, there **5** _____ .

Rebecca: Let's **6** _____ . They're old!

Tim: Hey, we can't afford new ones, I'm **7** _____ . These lamps are fine!

Rebecca: Yes, you're right.

Tim: Is that a bookcase?

Rebecca: No, it's a **8** _____ , but there are **9** _____ books here. Look!

Tim: Not really my **10** _____ of books. Hey, there's my favorite DVD.

Rebecca: But there isn't a DVD **11** _____ .

Extra challenge!

8 ★★★ Find four more differences between this room and the one in Exercise 1.

1 *In the first picture, there are some books. In this picture, there aren't any books.*

2 _____

_____

3 _____

_____

4 _____

_____

5 _____

_____

Grammar: Prepositions of place: *in, on, under, behind, in front of, next to*

3 mirror

7 notebook

5 video games

4 backpack

2 cell phone

6 bed

1 DVD player

1 ★ Look and circle the correct words.

There's a DVD player **1** *in / behind / (under)* the bed. My cell phone is **2** *in / in front of / behind* my backpack. There's a mirror on the wall **3** *in / next to / under* the window. My backpack is on the floor **4** *behind / in / in front of* the desk. There are some video games **5** *in / on / under* the chair, and my bed is **6** *in front of / behind / under* the dresser. My notebook is on the desk **7** *next to / under / behind* the computer.

2 ★★ Look and say where things are.

1 CD player / window

   The CD player's under the window.

2 poster / wall

   _____

3 lamp / computer

   _____

4 books / bed

   _____

5 bed / dresser

   _____

6 wastebasket / desk

   _____

3 ★★ **Where's the CD? Look at the pictures and write sentences using words from the box.**

> • the armchair • the chair • the dresser
> • the clock • the floor • the mirror
> • ~~the wastebasket~~

1 *The CD's in the wastebasket.*

2 _____
_____

3 _____
_____

4 _____
_____

5 _____
_____

Use your English: Make and respond to requests

4 ★ **Complete the conversations with the words and phrases from the box.**

> • borrow your • ~~Can I borrow~~ • course
> • I'm sorry • I need • no problem
> • please • Yes, sure

1 A: Hi, John. **1** *Can I borrow* your book?
   B: Yes, **2** _____ .

2 A: Mary, can I **3** _____ MP3 player?
   B: **4** _____ .

3 A: Mr. Smith, can I borrow a pen, **5** _____?
   B: Of **6** _____ .

4 A: Gina, can I borrow your cell phone?
   B: No, **7** _____ . **8** _____ it.

Consolidation

5 **Circle the correct answers below.**

A: What's wrong?

B: My cell phone's here, but I don't know where.

A: Is it **1**  the desk?

B: No, it isn't.

A: What about **2** 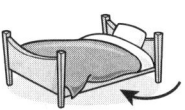 the bed?

B: No, not there.

A: Er . . . **3** the wastebasket?

B: Of course not!

A: What's that **4**  the dresser?

B: It's my MP3 player.

A: What? Your MP3 player's **5**  the floor?

What's **6**  the chair?

B: A book. Hey, wait a minute! **7** ? borrow your phone?

A: Yes, **8** ✔. Why?

B: I can call my phone . . . Listen!

It's **9**  my backpack.

1 ⓐ on	b) in	c) under
2 a) in	b) behind	c) under
3 a) under	b) in front of	c) in
4 a) next to	b) in	c) behind
5 a) on	b) in	c) under
6 a) on	b) under	c) in front of
7 a) I can	b) Can you	c) Can I
8 a) I'm sorry	b) course	c) sure
9 a) on	b) in	c) behind

Houses

INTEGRATED
CONSOLIDATION
SKILLS

Before you read

1 Before you read, check the meanings of these words.

> **New words**
> • downstairs • neighbors • noisy
> • quiet • townhouse • upstairs

Read

2 ★ Read and match Melissa and Sean to the photos of their houses.

1 My name's Melissa.
I live in a very
nice townhouse in
Philadelphia with my
brother and my parents.
Our townhouse is in
the middle of the
building. There are

Melissa

three bedrooms, a living room, and a
small kitchen. There isn't a garage, but there's
a small garden. The neighbors here are very
friendly. My bedroom isn't very big, but it's nice.

2 My name's Sean.
I live with my brother,
sister, and parents in a
semi-detached house
in north London. It's a
big house. There are
four bedrooms, a living
room, and a dining

Sean

room. There are two bathrooms, one upstairs
and one downstairs. There's a garage. The
road's sometimes noisy; but there's a garden
in front of the house, and the house is quiet.

A

B

C

D

3 ★ Read the descriptions again and complete the table.

	Melissa's house	Sean's house
Where?	1	North London
Type?	townhouse	4
Rooms?	2	5
Garage?	3	6
Garden?	yes	7

Listen

4 ★ 🎧 4 Listen to the conversation. Decide which picture on page 24 is Jackie's house.

5 ★★ 🎧 4 Listen again. Are these sentences true (T) or false (F)?

1 Jackie's from the U.S. $\boxed{T}$

2 It's Jackie's second time in Lima. ☐

3 Maya lives in a semi-detached house. ☐

4 Jackie lives in an apartment. ☐

5 There are five bathrooms in Jackie's house. ☐

6 There isn't a dining room in Jackie's house. ☐

7 There's a computer in Maya's bedroom. ☐

Jackie

Maya

Write

Writing tip: Punctuation

Remember! Use punctuation to make your writing clear.

- Use a **period** at the end of a sentence. Start a new sentence with a **capital letter**. *Upstairs there are three bedrooms and a bathroom. There isn't a porch.*
- Use a **comma** to join a list of three or more things. *There's a living room, a dining room, and a kitchen on the first floor.*
- Use a **question mark** at the end of a question. *How many bedrooms are there?*
- Use an **exclamation mark** at the end of surprising or funny sentences. *All my things are on the floor!*

6 ★ Find the mistakes in punctuation and capitalization and correct them.

1 my room isn't very big. There's a bed,	*My*
2 a bookcase a dresser, and a desk.	*bookcase, a*
3 There is a computer on the desk It is a	
4 very new computer. Next to the Computer	
5 there is a lamp. There is a wastebasket. under	
6 the desk. there is paper in the wastebasket.	
7 There are lots of books in the bookcase,	
8 There are books by J.K. Rowling. J.R. Tolkien,	
9 Roald Dahl, and Robert E. Howard?	
10 there aren't any televisions in the room.	
11 What's your favorite room! Why is it	
12 your Favorite room?	

7 ★★ Write about your room in your notebook. Use Exercise 6 to help you.

I have a brother.

Vocabulary: Family

1 ★ **Look at Dan's family tree. Label the people with words from the box.**

• aunt • cousin • father • grandfather • grandmother • mother • nephew • niece • sister • uncle

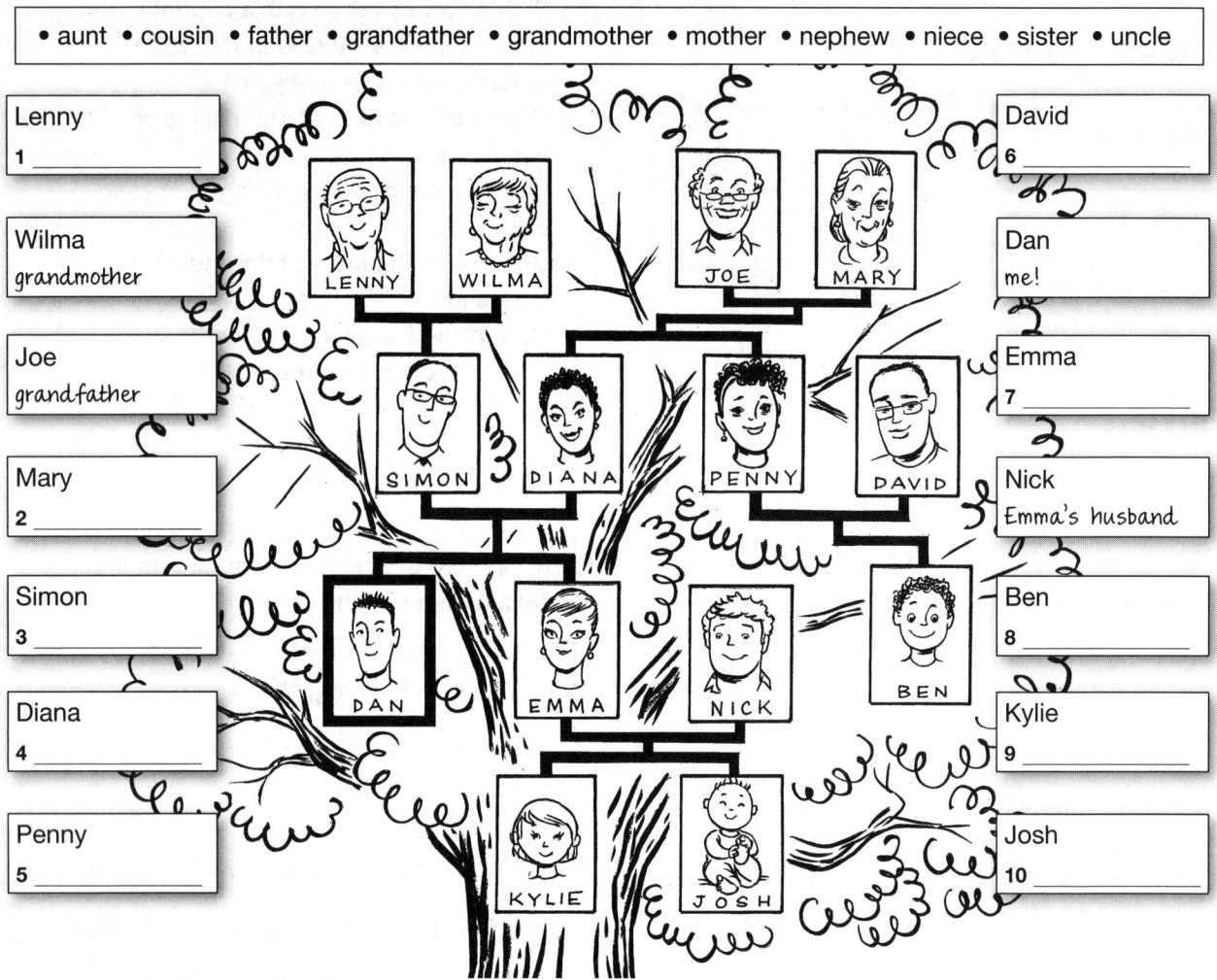

Lenny
1 _____

Wilma
grandmother

Joe
grandfather

Mary
2 _____

Simon
3 _____

Diana
4 _____

Penny
5 _____

David
6 _____

Dan
me!

Emma
7 _____

Nick
Emma's husband

Ben
8 _____

Kylie
9 _____

Josh
10 _____

2 ★★ **Who is it?**

1 I'm Dan's sister.   *Emma* _____

2 I'm Penny's husband. _____

3 Penny and Diana   _____ *and* _____
   are our children.

4 Dan is our uncle.   _____ *and* _____

5 I'm Lenny's wife.   _____

6 Dan is my cousin.   _____

7 David is my husband. _____

8 I'm Nick's son.   _____

9 I'm Emma's daughter. _____

Grammar: *Have* with *I, you, we, they*

3 ★ Complete the sentences with the correct form of *have* (+ affirmative or – negative).

Malcolm in the Middle is my favorite TV program. It's great! Lois and Hal are the parents. They **1** (+) *have* five children, all boys. Malcolm is in the middle of the family. They each **2** (+) _____ four brothers! Malcolm and his family **3** (–) _____ a last name. Well, they **4** (+) _____ a last name, but we don't know it. Malcolm's parents **5** (+) _____ a big family, but they **6** (–) _____ a lot of friends. I want the DVD. We **7** (+) _____ a lot of DVDs, but we **8** (–) _____ that one.

4 ★★ Complete the interview with Malcolm.

1 *Do you have* any brothers?
  Yes, *I have. I have four brothers*.
2 _____ any sisters?
  No, _____ .
3 _____ a wife?
  No, _____ .
4 _____ lots of friends?
  No, _____ . _____
  _____ one friend, Stevie.
5 _____ you and your brothers
  _____ children?
  No, _____ .
6 _____ your parents _____
  a big family?
  Yes, _____ .

Use your English: Talk about your family

5 ★ Match questions (1–4) to answers (a–d).
1 How many brothers do you have? [d]
2 How old is your father? [ ]
3 Do you have any cousins? [ ]
4 How old are they? [ ]

a) He's 53.
b) Yes, I do. I have three.
c) They're 12, 14, and 16.
d) I don't have any. I'm an only child.

Consolidation

6 Complete the letter with words from the box.

- children • children • ~~have~~ • have • How
- grandparents • many • men • nephew
- sister • wife • women

Dear Maria,

Yes, I **1** _have_ a big family. There are five **2** _____ : my father, two uncles, and two grandfathers. There are seven **3** _____ : my mother, four aunts, and two grandmothers. There are also lots of **4** _____ _____ . I have two brothers, José and Julio, and a **5** _____ , Camila. José is 14, Camila is 16, and Julio is 27! Julio's **6** _____ is Alejandra. She's 25 years old. They have two **7** _____ : a girl, Marisa, and a boy, Raul. So I'm an aunt! My niece and **8** _____ are fantastic!

My **9** _____ are in their seventies.

Do you **10** _____ any brothers or sisters? **11** _____ old are they? How **12** _____ cousins do you have?

Write soon,
Daniela

4B She has brown eyes.

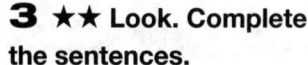

Phrases

1 ★ **Complete the conversation with phrases from the box.**

> • In your dreams. • Like me! • Oh, you know.
> • That's my kind of • ~~What's playing~~

Will: **1** *What's playing* at the movies this week?

Chloe: A new Brad Pitt movie.

Will: Oh great. **2** _____ movie.

Chloe: He's very good-looking.

Will: **3** _____

Chloe: **4** _____

Will: What? What do you mean?

Chloe: Well, you're nice-looking, but you're not Brad. You're more like Ben Stiller.

Will: Who?

Chloe: **5** _____ He's in *Night at the Museum*, *Meet the Parents* . . .

Will: Oh, him. Really?

Chloe: Yes, dark hair, brown eyes, nice looking.

Will: Thanks!

Vocabulary: Appearance

2 ★ **Look at the picture. Circle the correct words.**

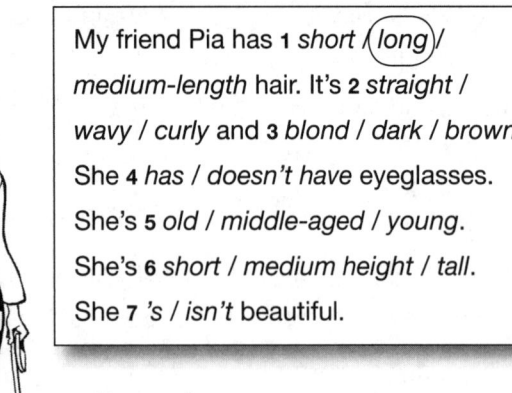

> My friend Pia has **1** *short / (long) / medium-length* hair. It's **2** *straight / wavy / curly* and **3** *blond / dark / brown*. She **4** *has / doesn't have* eyeglasses. She's **5** *old / middle-aged / young*. She's **6** *short / medium height / tall*. She **7** *'s / isn't* beautiful.

3 ★★ Look. Complete the sentences.

This is my Uncle Peter.

1 *He has short, dark* hair.

2 _____ eyeglasses.

3 _____ a moustache.

4 _____ a beard.

5 _____ -aged.

6 _____ very tall.

7 _____ height.

8 I think _____ good-looking.

Grammar: *Has* with *he, she, it*

4 ★ **Look at the table and the text about Ryan. Complete the sentences about Bria and Matt.**

	Ryan	Bria	Matt
Brothers?	1	1	0
Sisters?	0	2	1
Nieces?	0	0	1
Cousins?	4	1	0

Ryan has a brother. He doesn't have any sisters. He doesn't have any nieces. He has four cousins.

Bria **1** *has* a brother. **2** _____ two sisters. **3** _____ any nieces. **4** _____ one cousin.

Matt **5** _____ any brothers. He **6** _____ one sister.

5 ★★ Use the prompts to ask and answer questions about the people in Exercise 4.

1 Ryan / brothers?

Does Ryan have any brothers?

Yes, he has. He has one brother.

2 Matt / nieces?

_____

_____

_____

3 Bria / nieces?

_____

_____

4 Matt / sisters?

_____

_____

5 Bria / cousins?

_____

_____

_____

Consolidation

6 Circle the correct answers.

Luciana: Hi, Debbie.

Debbie: Hello? Luciana? Where are you? In Italy?

Luciana: No. I'm in Spain, at a language school.

Debbie: Oh, wow! 1 *Do you have* a good place to live?

Luciana: Yes. 2 _____ a room in Barcelona.

Debbie: Are the other students nice?

Luciana: Well, there's one Italian boy. His name's Paolo. He's 15. He's very 3 _____ and he 4 _____ short, black hair. He 5 _____ very good-looking. My best friend in the course is Melina. She's from Greece. She has 6 _____ , black hair and glasses. She's quite short, 7 _____ me.

Debbie: Who's the teacher?

Luciana: His name's Mark. He's 8 _____ . About 50. He's medium 9 _____ and he's very friendly. So, can you come to Barcelona to see me?

Debbie: Of course. On Friday evening. We can go to the movies. What's 10 _____ ?

Luciana: I don't know. I can look.

Debbie: OK. See you on Friday.

1 a) Are you   b) Do you have   c) You have
2 a) I'd   b) I'm   c) I have
3 a) high   b) height   c) tall
4 a) has   b) is   c) have
5 a) has   b) 's   c) have
6 a) wave   b) waved   c) wavy
7 a) like   b) same   c) as
8 a) middle-ages b) middle-age   c) middle-aged
9 a) high   b) tall   c) height
10 a) play   b) playing   c) played

Extra challenge!

7 ★★★ Think of a famous person. Write a description of him or her in your notebook. Use Exercise 2 to help you.

• name of the person
• hair
• eyes
• glasses / beard / moustache?
• age
• height
• good-looking / beautiful?

4c When's your birthday?

Vocabulary: Months and ordinal numbers

1 ★ Complete the months of the year.

1 *January*   5 M*ay*   9 S*eptember*
2 F_____   6 J*une*   10 O_____
3 M_____   7 J_____   11 N_____
4 A_____   8 A_____   12 D_____

2 ★★ Write the dates in words.

Our birthdays
English class
Summer course

1 Gianna 1/3   *the third of January*
2 Julia 2/20   _____
3 Takara 3/22   _____
4 Aslan 4/24   _____
5 Huan 5/18   _____
6 Rania 6/5   _____
7 Stefan 7/31   _____
8 Karol 8/12   _____

Vocabulary: Seasons

3 ★ Write the seasons.

1 _____   2 _____

3 _____   4 _____

Grammar: Prepositions of time: *in, on*

4 ★ Complete the information with *in* or *on*.

My zodiac sign is Taurus. My birthday is **1** ____ the spring. It's **2** ____ May. It's **3** ____ May 16. This year, it's **4** ____ a Saturday.

5 ★★ Now write about three more people.

Zodiac sign: Aquarius
Season: winter
Date: 2/10
Day this year: Tuesday

My zodiac sign is Aquarius. _____
_____
_____
_____

Zodiac sign: Libra
Season: fall
Date: 10/14
Day this year: Wednesday

_____
_____
_____

Zodiac sign: Leo
Season: summer
Date: 8/3
Day this year: Monday

_____
_____
_____
_____

6 ★★ Answer the questions below. Write out the dates in words.

NOVEMBER **18**
My birthday

English test
WEDNESDAY

28 FRIDAY

29 SATURDAY Claire's party

Summer Music Festival

School trip 10/7

1 A: When's the music festival?

B: *It's in the summer.*

2 A: When's your English test?

B: _____

3 A: When's the school trip?

B: _____

4 A: When's your birthday?

B: _____

5 A: When's Claire's party?

B: _____

Consolidation

7 Circle the correct answers.

Ruby: Hey, look at this. A website with famous people's birthdays on it. We can see who has the same birthday as we do. When's your birthday?

Josh: My birthday's **1** *on* the **2** _____ of May.

Ruby: Let's see. Cate Blanchett, George Lucas—cool, Tim Roth.

Josh: So, when's your birthday?

Ruby: August **3** _____ . Neil Armstrong has the same birthday as I do.

Josh: Who?

Ruby: The first man on the moon. That was **4** _____1969. "One small step for man . . ."

Josh: Great! OK, let's do something else. You say a famous person, and I say the zodiac sign. I'm good at zodiac signs.

Ruby: OK, George Clooney.

Josh: George Clooney. I think he's Taurus. Cool and good-looking—**5** _____ me!

Ruby: That's Taurus?

Josh: Yes. Taurus is the cool zodiac sign. I'm Taurus.

Ruby: When is Taurus?

Josh: It's **6** _____ the spring. April and May. I think it's from April **7** _____ to May **8** _____ .

Ruby: You're right. Amazing. His birthday is **9** _____ of May.

Josh: See. Look at other famous Taurus stars. They're all cool.

Ruby: Wait a minute. Here we are. Jack Nicholson, Uma Thurman, Harvey Keitel . . . You're right! Cool and good-looking.

1 a) at	b) on	c) in
2 a) four	b) fourteenth	c) fortieth
3 a) five	b) the five	c) fifth
4 a) in	b) on	c) at
5 a) as	b) like	c) same
6 a) on	b) in	c) at
7 a) twenty-two	b) twentieth-two	c) twenty-second
8 a) on the twenty-first	b) the twenty-one	c) twenty-first
9 a) in the sixth	b) on the sixth	c) at the sixth

4D Curriculum link: Science

The Johansson twins

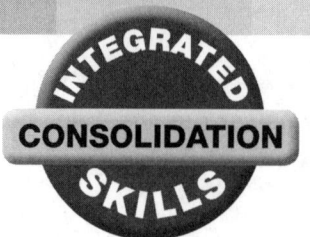

INTEGRATED CONSOLIDATION SKILLS

Read

Learning strategy: Guess the meaning of new words

Remember! When you read, don't stop when you see a new or difficult word. Try to guess its meaning from the words and phrases near that word. If you still don't know the meaning of the word, use a dictionary.

1 ★ Skim the article about Scarlett Johansson and check (✓) the people in her family.

a) Danny	☐	d) Vanessa	☐
b) Hunter	☐	e) Adrian	☐
c) Arnold	☐	f) Christian	☐

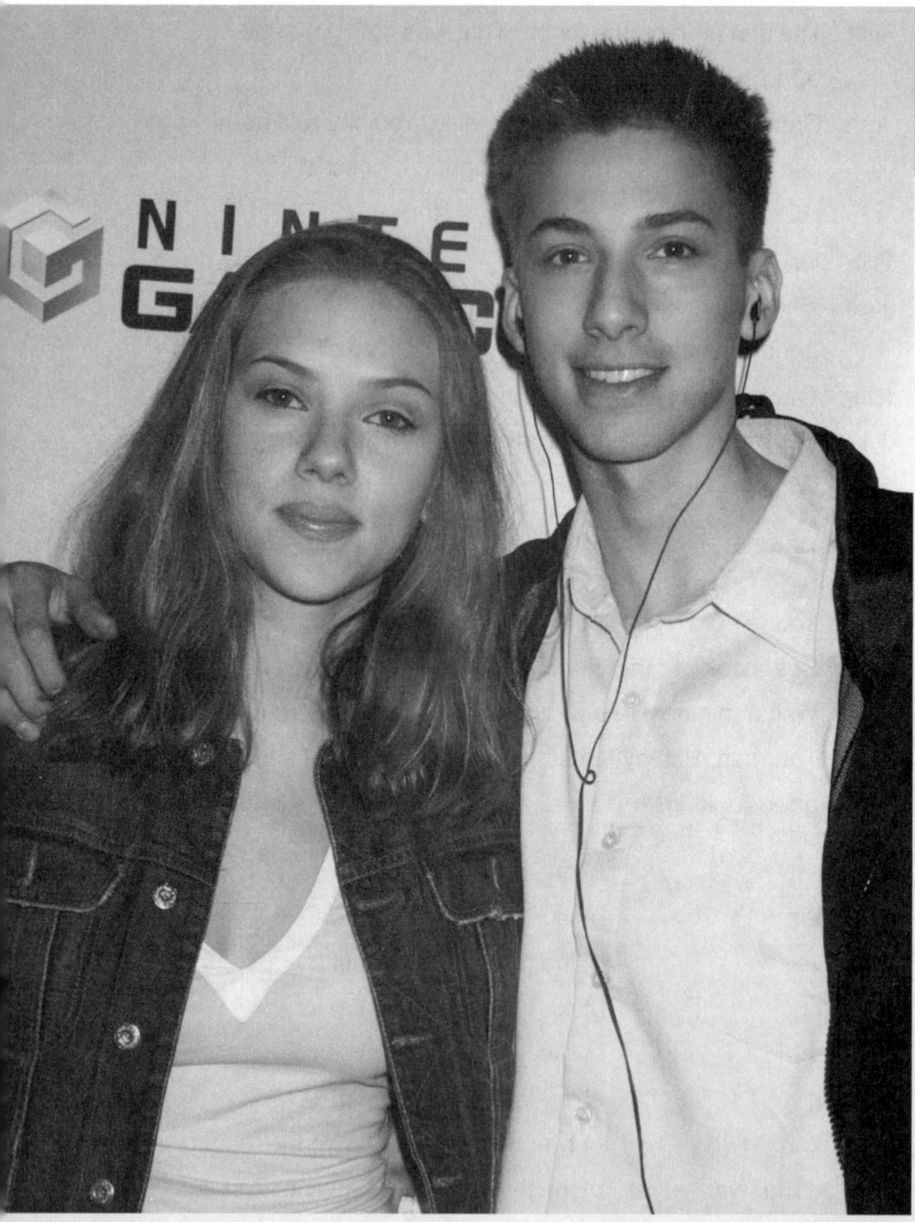

Scarlett Johansson is an American actress from New York.

Her mother's from New York, but her father's from Denmark. Her birthday's on the twenty-second of November. She has two brothers, Adrian and Hunter. She has a sister, Vanessa, and a step-brother, Christian. Hunter is her twin. They aren't identical. Scarlett says they're like Danny DeVito and Arnold Schwarzenegger in the film *Twins*! Hunter's six-foot three, and Scarlett's five-foot three! When people see them, they don't believe that they're related. They're very different. She's short, he's tall. She has naturally red hair (but it's often blond). He has dark hair. He wears glasses, and she doesn't. Some people think Hunter's her new boyfriend!

2 ★★ Read the article again and answer the questions.

1 Where is Scarlett from?

She's from New York.

2 When is her birthday?

_____

_____

3 How many brothers and sisters does she have?

_____

_____

4 What is her twin brother's name?

_____

_____

5 How is she different from her twin?

a) _____

_____

b) _____

_____

c) _____

_____

3 ★★ Read the article again and circle the correct meaning for the boldfaced words.

1 **step-brother**

   a) a brother in a different country

   b) a boy whose parent is married to one

      of your parents

   c) a man married to your sister

2 **identical**

   a) different

   b) similar

   c) exactly the same

3 **related**

   a) from the same family

   b) friends

   c) the same nationality

4 **naturally red**

   a) a dark red color

   b) the natural color

   c) a beautiful color

Listen

4 ★ (5) Listen to the conversation and circle the correct words.

1 Angela and Simon *are / aren't* brother and sister.

2 Simon is *different from / identical to* his twin brother.

3 Jenna and Barbara have a *brother / father* named George.

4 Jenna and Barbara *are / aren't* identical.

5 Alanis Morisette is *Canadian / American*.

6 Mary-Kate and Ashley's last name is *Olsen / Olson*.

Write

5 ★ Read the notes about twins Joel and Benji Madden. Write about them in your notebook, using the ideas about the Phelps twins on page 37 of the Student Book to help you.

Joel and Benji Madden are musicians in the band

Good Charlotte. They are twins . . .

Name: Joel Madden
Job: singer
Band: Good Charlotte
Twin: Benji
Identical: Yes
Favorite sport: Baseball
Favorite team: The Baltimore Orioles
Favorite movie: *Star Wars*

Name: Benji Madden
Job: guitarist
Band: Good Charlotte
Twin: Joel
Identical: Yes
Favorite sport: Baseball
Favorite team: The Baltimore Orioles
Favorite movie: *The Boondock Saints*
(It's about twins!)

I don't work here.

Vocabulary: Occupations

1 ★ Unscramble the letters to make jobs.

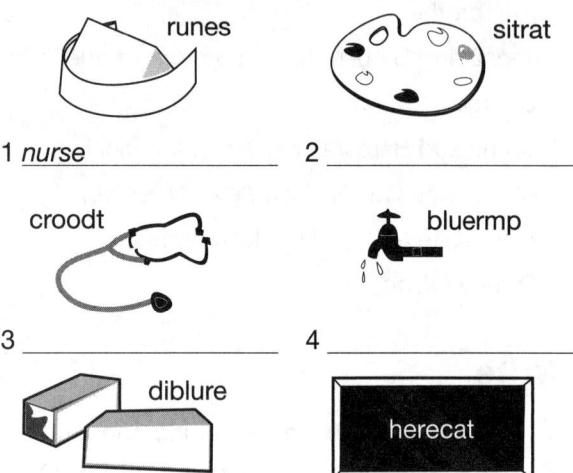

runes

sitrat

1 *nurse* _____

2 _____

croodt

bluermp

3 _____

4 _____

diblure

herecat

5 _____

6 _____

Phrases

2 ★ Circle the correct answers.

1 A: This is my sister Nadia. She has a new job!

B: *Cool!*

a) Don't look at me!   (b) Cool!   c) OK, guys.

2 _____, do you want to hear

about it?

a) OK, guys   b) Very funny   c) Cool

3 A: Nadia works as a waitress on Saturdays!

B: Really? Can I have a burger and soda, please?

A: _____

a) Don't look at me!   b) OK, guys.   c) Very funny!

4 A: It's an Italian restaurant. Ask Nadia in Italian!

B: _____ I don't speak Italian.

a) Cool!   b) Don't look at me!   c) Very funny!

5 A: My brother has a new job, too, as a disc jockey.

B: Wow! _____ That's great.

a) Very funny!   b) OK, guys.   c) Cool!

3 ★★ Use the sentences (a–h) to make conversations for each picture.

1 A: ☐ f | *Wow! Look! An e-mail from Brad Pitt!*

B: ☐ c | *Very funny!* _____

2 A: ☐ _____

B: ☐ _____

3 A: ☐ _____

B: ☐ _____

4 A: ☐ _____

B: ☐ _____

a) I have a great car. A 1998 Cadillac!

b) OK, guys. Here we are.

c) Very funny!

d) Don't look at me! I don't know.

e) Cool!

f) Wow! Look! An e-mail from Brad Pitt!

g) Great! Can we have a drink of water now?

h) What's the answer to number three?

Grammar: Simple present with *I, you, we, they*

4 ★ **Make sentences. Use the simple present of the verbs in parentheses.**

1 We *live* (live) in Chile.

2 _____ (you / work) here?

3 No, I _____ (do). I'm not from this town.

4 "Do you and your friends study German at school?" "No, _____ (do)."

5 What languages _____ (they / speak)?

6 Magali and Yolanda _____ (be) from São Paulo.

7 My friends and I _____ (not work). We go to school.

8 "Do your friends in Mexico study English?" "Yes, _____ (do)."

5 ★★ **A famous South American musician is talking to some fans. Complete the conversation. Use the correct form of the verbs.**

live

Fan: **1** *Do* you *live* in a big house?

Musician: No, I **2** _____ . I **3** _____ in a small apartment. I'm not a big star! My apartment's in Rio de Janeiro.

Fan: Where **4** _____ you _____ in Rio?

be

Musician: In Centro. It's a great place.

Fan: Where **5** _____ your parents from? Brazil?

Musician: No. They **6** _____ from Argentina. I am Argentinian.

study

Fan: Your English is very good.

Musician: Thank you. In South America, we **7** _____ English at school. **8** _____ you _____ Spanish in your school?

Fan: No, we **9** _____ . We **10** _____ French and English.

Consolidation

6 **Complete the chat with words and phrases from the box.**

> • are you from • Are your parents
> • do you speak • doctors • don't • don't live
> • don't speak • study • very funny
> • Where do you live • work • you speak

DJ Bob: Hi, guys.

Nero: Hi, Bob. Are you really a DJ?

DJ Bob: Hi, Nero. No, I'm not. I go to school. I'm 15.

Nero: Where **1** *are you from* ?

DJ Bob: Quebec.

Nero: Quebec? Cool. You're American. ☺

DJ Bob: What?! No way! Quebec's in Canada, not the U.S.

Nero: ☺ Sorry. So, do **2** _____ French?

DJ Bob: Yes, of course. My parents **3** _____ _____ English at home, just French. At school, we **4** _____ in French! **5** _____ , Nero?

Nero: I live in Buenos Aires. It's a big city.

DJ Bob: Buenos Aires? So, **6** _____ Portuguese? ☺

Nero: Ha, ha, **7** _____ . No, I **8** _____ . I **9** _____ in Brazil. I live in Argentina!

DJ Bob: **10** _____ from Argentina?

Nero: Yes, they are. They **11** _____ in a big hospital here in Buenos Aires. They're **12** _____ .

Grammar: Simple present with *he, she, it*

1 ★ Complete the article with the correct form of the verbs.

Basel

SWITZERLAND

SOUTH AFRICA

Roger Federer

Roger Federer **1** *is* (be) from Basel in Switzerland.

His first language is German, but he

2 _____ (speak) very good English. Why?

His mother **3** _____ (speak) English.

His mother **4** _____ (not be)

from Switzerland. She is South African.

5 _____ Roger _____ (speak) a third language?

Yes, he does. He **6** _____ (speak) French.

7 _____ Roger _____ (work) in a hospital

or a school? No, he **8** _____ (not work)

inside. He **9** _____ (work) outside.

He is a tennis player.

2 ★★ **Read about Juan Morales. Then rewrite the text using *his* and *he*.**

> **1** My name is Juan Morales. **2** Where do I live?
> **3** I live in Barcelona, but I'm from Madrid.
> **4** I don't work in an office. **5** What do I do? **6** I'm a photographer. **7** I take photographs of people.
> **8** I don't want to live in Spain. **9** I want to live in Los Angeles. **10** It's my favorite place!

1 *His name is Juan Morales.* _____

2 Where _____

3 _____

4 _____

5 _____

6 _____

7 _____

8 _____

9 _____

10 _____

Vocabulary: Places of work

3 ★ **Write *on* or *in* by the place of work.**

_on_ 1 a construction site

____ 2 a hospital

____ 3 a mall

____ 4 an office

____ 5 a restaurant

____ 6 a school

____ 7 the sidewalk

____ 8 a store

4 ★★ Write where the people work.

1 Tom's a chef.

   He works in a restaurant.

2 You're a secretary.

   _____

3 My mother's a teacher.

   _____

4 I'm a builder.

   I_____

5 Kevin's a salesclerk.

   _____

6 My brothers are plumbers.

   _____

Consolidation

5 Complete the Internet chat with words from the box.

> • does • go   goes • in • in • is • is • live
> • speak • speaks • studies • to

```
⊝ ○ ○

Becks says: Hi. I'm in Spain with Maria.

Cath1 says: Hi Becks. Does Maria 1 speak
English?

Becks says: Yes. She 2 _____ very good
English. ☺

Cath1 says: Where 3 _____ Maria from?

Becks says: Galicia. Her father 4 _____
a waiter. He works 5 _____ a big restaurant.

Cath1 says: Cool. Does Maria 6 _____
in a nice house?

Becks says: Yes, she 7 _____ .

Cath1 says: Where does she 8 _____
to school?

Becks says: She 9 _____ to school in
Orense. She 10 _____ three languages at
school: French, Italian, and English!

Cath1 says: Wow! Does Maria want 11 _____
work in a restaurant?

Becks says: No, she wants to work 12 _____
an office.
```

Extra challenge!

6 ★★★ Read the profile. Complete the questions. Then answer the questions with full sentences.

Name:	Melanie Aquino
Born:	Quito, Ecuador
Lives now:	New York, U.S.
Job:	Doctor
Place of work:	Hospital near Central Park
Languages:	English, Spanish, Portuguese

1 What / name?

   What's her name?

   Her name's Melanie Aquino.

2 Where / from?

   _____

   _____

3 Where / live now?

   _____

   _____

4 What / do?

   _____

   _____

5 Where / work?

   _____

   _____

6 speak / French?

   _____

   _____

7 speak / Spanish?

   _____

   _____

5c I love him.

Grammar: Object pronouns: *me, you, him, her, it, us, them*

1 ★ Match comments (a–e) to pictures (1–5).

Julia Roberts
1 e

Brad Pitt
2 ☐

potato chips
3 ☐

soccer
4 ☐

you and me
5 ☐

a) We love it.
b) I love them.
c) I like him.
d) I love you, and you love me.
e) I don't like her.

2 ★ Complete the sentences with object pronouns.

1 My brother's nice. I like *him* .

2 Burgers are disgusting. I don't like _____ .

3 My mom's great. I love _____ .

4 This sandwich is very old. I don't want _____ .

5 We're good students. Our teacher likes _____ .

6 My sister takes my CDs. She doesn't ask _____ .

7 What's your cell phone number? I want to text ____ .

3 ★★ Complete the text with subject pronouns or object pronouns.

| TV | Movies | Sports | School | Food | Music |

Food

What do **1** *you* like to eat? We want to hear from
2 _____ ! E-mail

Readers' opinions

Karen, aged 13, San Francisco, California

I don't eat fast food. I don't like **3** _____ .

People ask **4** _____ : "Do you eat potato

chips?" and **5** _____ say: "No, I don't like

6 _____ . **7** _____ 're disgusting." My

best friend, Melanie, is the same. **8** _____ 's

great. I really like **9** _____ . Our friends don't

ask **10** _____ to go to the food court with

them. **11** _____ don't like the food that they

like. My brother's different. He loves burgers and

soda. I don't go out to eat with **12** _____ !

Vocabulary: Adjectives of opinion

4 ★ Circle the correct words.

1 I don't like potato chips. They're (awful)/ cool.

2 Sam likes Jim Carrey. He thinks he's
   weird / funny.

3 We love Daniel Craig. He's *terrible / cool*.

4 Joe hates soda. He thinks it's *terrible / good*.

5 Sofia loves Dan Radcliffe. She thinks he's
   incredible / boring.

6 I like the new James Bond movie. It's *bad / good*.

7 My parents don't like rap music. They think it's
   weird / awesome.

8 We love the Beckhams. We think they're
   terrible / great.

5 ★★ **Read the e-mail and answer the questions below.**

```
○ ○ ○                Mail
```

Hi Alex,
I have a new DVD. It's *Avatar*! I love James Cameron's movies. Have you seen *Titanic*? Cameron directed that movie, too. I loved it! Leonardo DiCaprio was incredible— and Kate Winslet was, too! And I think Zoe Saldana will be a big star—just from her performance in *Avatar*! She is a great actor! I really like her. I'm not sure about *Aliens*. It was a little weird. It won awards, but I think the acting was terrible! But, all in all, Cameron is an amazing director. I want to see his new movies. I hear there's one with the Black-Eyed Peas.
Beth

What does Beth think of . . .

1 *Avatar* and *Titanic*?
She *loves them* .

2 Leonardo DiCaprio and Kate Winslet?
She thinks _____ .

3 Zoe Saldana?
She _____ .

4 *Aliens*?
She _____ .

5 The acting in *Aliens*?
She _____ .

6 James Cameron?
She thinks _____ .

Use your English: Exchange opinions

6 ★ **Circle the correct words.**

1 This is a good book. I (*like*)/ *don't like* it.

2 That's a bad idea. I *want* / *don't want* to do it.

3 What an awful movie! I *want* / *don't want* to buy the DVD.

4 This is a great video game. *Can I borrow it?* / *I don't want it.*

5 What a weird song! I *don't like* / *love* it.

6 This is terrible food. I *want* / *don't want* to eat here again.

7 Tennis is great. I *love* / *hate* it.

8 A: Is the movie funny?
B: Yes, it is. It's very *good* / *bad*.

9 This house is really cool. I *like* / *don't like* it.

10 A: Your cell phone is amazing.
B: Yes, it's *new and expensive* / *old and difficult to use.*

Consolidation

7 **Use the cues to answer the questions. Use one word in each blank. Contractions count as one word.**

1 Do you like this song?
don't / hate / terrible
No , *I* *don't* . *I* *hate* *it* . *It's* *terrible* .

2 What do you think of me?
like / cool
_____ _____ _____ . _____ _____ !

3 Do you like Johnny Depp?
do / love / incredible
_____ , _____ _____ . _____ _____
_____ . _____ _____ !

4 Do you like youth clubs?
don't / hate / awful
_____ , _____ _____ . _____ _____
_____ . _____ _____ !

5 What do you think about Angelina Jolie?
not sure / cool / weird
I'm _____ _____ about _____ .
_____ _____ , but _____ _____ !

Problems at work

INTEGRATED
CONSOLIDATION
SKILLS

Before you read

1 Before you read, check the meanings of these words.

> **New words**
> • agree (*v.*) • alarm • angry • bus stop • busy
> • decide • grocery (store) • help (*v., n.*) • late
> • lazy • see (*v.*)

Read

2 ★ Match each text (A–C) with the correct final sentence (1–3). Then complete each sentence with the correct name.

1 _____ gets to work 30 minutes late, and the manager is angry. ☐

2 _____ looks for a job in a different restaurant. ☐

3 _____ hates the job in the supermarket, but his uncle doesn't want him in his store now. ☐

3 ★★ Read the texts again. Are these sentences true (T) or false (F)?

1 Roland doesn't like his uncle. [F]

2 Roland's uncle has a big supermarket. ☐

3 Roland doesn't work in his uncle's store. ☐

4 Jenny works on Saturdays. ☐

5 Jenny's cell phone doesn't work. ☐

6 Jenny's bus is late. ☐

7 Kieran is hard-working. ☐

8 Kieran tells Glenn it is a good job. ☐

9 Kieran doesn't like Glenn. ☐

B Jenny is a waitress on Saturdays. One week, she goes out to the mall with her friends. She doesn't have an alarm on her cell phone, and she forgets the time. When she looks at her phone, she sees that she is late for work. She telephones the manager from the mall and says that she is at the bus stop near her house, and there is a problem with the buses.

A Roland's uncle has a small grocery store. He is very busy and needs help. Roland likes his uncle and agrees to work with him on Saturdays, but then sees a job in a big supermarket. The supermarket pays good money, and Roland's uncle doesn't. Roland decides to work in the supermarket. On his first day at work for his uncle, he goes to the supermarket instead and doesn't tell his uncle. His uncle is very angry.

Listen

> **Learning strategy: Predict from the task**
> **Remember!** Look at the task before you listen.
> Try to predict some of the words you might hear.
> This will help you understand more the first time
> you listen.

4 ★ 🎧 **6 Listen to the conversation and circle the correct answers.**

1 The three people . . .

  a) are friends.

  b) work at the same place.

  c) want the same job.

2 They are . . .

  a) at work.   b) at home.   c) at the mall.

3 The one thing that they DON'T talk about is . . .

  a) money.   b) school.   c) work.

4 The three people work on Saturdays. What day is it now?

  a) Sunday   b) Saturday   c) Friday

C Kieran works in a burger restaurant. He likes the job and works hard. The manager likes him and is very nice. There is a job ad on the door, and Kieran's friend, Glenn, wants to work there. Kieran knows that Glenn is lazy. Kieran likes Glenn, but he doesn't want to work with him. He tells Glenn that it is a terrible job and that the manager is awful.

5 ★★ 🎧 **6 Listen again and answer these questions. Write R (Roland), K (Kieran), or J (Jenny).**

Who . . .

1 works in a sporting goods store?   R

2 asks about money? ☐

3 has a new cell phone? ☐

4 asks about Glenn? ☐

5 knows where Glenn works? ☐

6 takes a bus to work? ☐

7 drinks a lot of soda at work? ☐

Write

6 ★ **Read about a problem Manuel has. Choose the best heading: a), b), or c).**

a) No friends, no job.
b) Two friends, one job.
c) One friend, two jobs.

> I work in a supermarket on Saturdays. It's called "Low Price Supermarket" and it's on Hefner Road in Oklahoma City. I get $5.50 an hour. They want a second person to work on Saturdays because there is a lot of work to do. The manager, Mr. Cuevo, wants an honest, hard-working, fit person aged 16 or older to work from 6 P.M.–10 P.M. on Saturdays. I have his phone number. It's 405-555-1234. What's my problem? My friends Jorgé and Paulo both want the job.

7 ★★ **Use the information in the text in Exercise 6 to write a paragraph of advice to Manuel in your notebook.**

What time does it start?

Phrases

1 ★ **Complete the conversation with words and phrases from the box.**

> • amazing • Oh, man! • Let's hurry!
> • welcome to

Announcer: Good afternoon and **1** *welcome to* today's game.

Will: Come on, Ben. It's five to three. The game starts at three o'clock.

Ben: Wait! Can we buy a program?

Will: Sure. Look! That's Ronaldo.

Ben: **2** _____

Will: He's an **3** _____ soccer player. We can stand here.

Ben: Here? I can't see. Can you lift me up?

Will: **4** _____ You're too old for that!

Vocabulary: Clock times

2 ★ **Write the times.**

1 *It's nine o'clock.* _____

2 _____

3 _____

4 _____

5 _____

6 _____

7 _____

8 _____

Grammar: Simple present with fixed times

3 ★ **Look at the planner and match the beginnings of the sentences (1–8) to the endings (a–h).**

> **16 MONDAY**
> English class: 5–6:30 P.M.
>
> **17 TUESDAY**
> School is over! 3:30 P.M.
> Hooray! Concert: 8:15–9:45 P.M.
>
> **18 WEDNESDAY**
> Bus to Grandma's:
> Boston 7:45 – Brookline 9:20
>
> **19 THURSDAY**
> Help in Grandma's store
> 9 A.M. – 5:30 P.M.
>
> **20 FRIDAY**
> Train home: Boston 10:35 – Brookline 11:55
> Movie: 6 P.M. – 8:30 P.M.
> Bus from movies: 8:40

1 My English class a) opens at nine o'clock.

2 The concert b) Boston at twenty-five to eleven.

3 The bus leaves c) ends at eight thirty.

4 The bus arrives d) starts at five o'clock.

5 Grandma's store e) starts at a quarter after eight.

6 The store closes f) Boston at a quarter to eight.

7 The train leaves g) in Brookline at twenty after nine.

8 The movie h) at five thirty.

Grammar: Preposition of time: *at*

4 ★ Write questions and answers.

1 What time / the English class / start? (5:00)

Q: *What time does the English class start?*

A: *It starts at five o'clock.*

2 What time / English class / end? (6:30)

Q: _____

A: _____

3 What time / the concert / end? (9:45)

Q: _____

A: _____

4 What time / the train / arrive in Brookline? (11:55)

Q: _____

A: _____

5 What time / the movie / start? (6:00)

Q: _____

A: _____

6 What time / the bus / leave the movies? (8:40)

Q: _____

A: _____

Consolidation

5 Circle the correct words.

Year 2010
Soccer game
3:45–5:15

Sat. exam help
School is open
from 9–12

End-of-year
disco
Friday
8:30–11 P.M.

School trip to Boston
THURSDAY
Bus at 6 A.M.!!
Arrives in Boston
about 9 A.M

http://www.park-school/webnews

Welcome **1** *on / for / to* our new website with all the news from our school!

The Year 2010 soccer game **2** *opens / starts / leaves* at quarter **3** *to / from / after* four on Friday and ends at quarter **4** *after / to / of* five.

Don't forget the end-of-year disco. There are some tickets, but hurry up and get one today! The disco is on Friday **5** *afternoon / morning / night*. It starts at eight **6** *fifteen / o'clock / thirty*.

The school is open for exam help this Saturday, but only for three hours. The session starts at nine o'clock **7** *in / on / at* the morning and ends at **8** *midnight / the afternoon / noon*.

Finally, there is a school trip to Boston on Thursday, but the bus **9** *arrives / leaves / starts* at 6 A.M.!

It arrives in Boston at about nine **10** *A.M. / O'CLOCK / P.M.* in the morning.

Extra challenge!

6 ★★★ Look at the T.V. listings and write about the programs.

Channel 1

6–6:30 The news

6:30–8:15 Soccer: Chelsea v. Los Angeles Galaxy

8:15–9:45 Movie: *Casablanca* (1941)

9:45–10:35 *Big Sister*

1 The news *starts at six o'clock and ends at six thirty.*

2 The soccer game _____

3 The movie, *Casablanca*, _____

4 *Big Sister* _____

Vocabulary: Daily routines

1 ★ Label the activities with a word or phrase from each box.

• brush • call • do • eat • eat • get • go • listen to • take • watch

• a friend • a shower • breakfast • home • lunch • music • school • TV • your homework • your teeth

1 *brush your teeth*

2 _____

3 _____

4 _____ to _____

5 _____

6 _____

7 _____

8 _____

9 _____

10 _____

Grammar: Adverbs of frequency

2 ★ Rewrite the sentences with the adverbs of frequency in the correct place.

1 I get up at ten o'clock. (never)
I never get up at ten o'clock.

2 We hardly watch TV. (ever)
_____

3 My parents eat pizza for lunch. (sometimes)
_____

4 My bedroom's cold. (always)
_____

5 I ever eat breakfast. (hardly)
_____

6 My friends don't call me. (often)
_____

3 ★★ Complete the answers to the questions using the words in parentheses.

1 What do you have for lunch?
(usually a sandwich)
I *usually have a sandwich for lunch.*

2 What time does your father get up?
(always / 6:45 A.M.)
He _____

3 Do you often get home at 3:30?
(hardly ever / at 3:30)
No, _____
_____

4 Does your sister go out after school?
(sometimes / the mall with her friends)
Yes, _____
_____

5 What do you do at night?
(usually / play video games)
I _____

6 Does your mother read in bed? (never)
No, she _____

4 ★★ **Write about the pictures using the words and phrases from the box. Use the correct form of the verbs.**

> • be late for school • cook Chinese food
> • drive to school • play video games • watch TV

1 me / always

I'm always late for school.

2 Mia and Kyle / never

_____

3 my brother / often

_____

4 my parents / sometimes

_____

5 our teacher / hardly ever

_____

Consolidation

5 **Circle the correct answers below.**

Ben is a very bad boy. He **1** _____ eats burgers and potato chips for breakfast. He **2** _____ does his homework. He's **3** _____ late for school, and he doesn't help around the house. He watches TV, and he always **4** _____ to bed late.

Gail is a very good girl. She **5** _____ late for school. When she gets **6** _____ home, she always does **7** _____ homework. She sometimes calls her friends, but not very **8** _____ . She always listens **9** _____ nice music, and she sometimes reads in **10** _____ .

1 a) always	b) never	c) doesn't
2 a) usually	b) never	c) often
3 a) hardly	b) never	c) often
4 a) goes	b) gets	c) is
5 a) never	b) is never	c) never is
6 a) to	b) at	c) –
7 a) her	b) his	c) your
8 a) never	b) often	c) usually
9 a) –	b) to	c) with
10 a) bedroom	b) chair	c) bed

Grammar: Adverbial expressions of frequency

1 ★ Match phrases (1–6) to phrases (a–f) that have the same meaning.

1 twice a day
2 once a year
3 twice a week
4 once a week
5 three times a week
6 once a month

a) every July
b) every Saturday and Sunday
c) every Monday, Tuesday, and Friday
d) every Sunday
e) every morning and night
f) the first of every month

2 ★★ Rewrite the sentences using phrases from the box.

• every five minutes • every Saturday
• once a year
• on Thursday, Friday, Saturday, and Sunday
• three times a day • twice a week

1 I go shopping once a week.
I go shopping *every Saturday* .

2 My father goes to Chile every September.
My father goes to Chile _____ .

3 I have English classes on Wednesday and Friday.
I have English classes _____ .

4 My mother drinks tea in the morning, in the afternoon, and at night.
My mother drinks tea _____

_____ .

5 I play video games four days a week.
I play video games_____ .

6 My friend texts 12 times an hour!
My friend texts _____ .

3 ★★ Ask and answer questions about the people in the pictures. Use the cues on page 47.

Amy	**Emma**
7 A.M. / 1 P.M. / 10 P.M.	M / T / W / T / F / S / S

Louisa	**Juan**
Sun / Sun / Sun / Sun	Mon / Tues / Wed / Thurs

Chris	**Maria and Mario**
Mon / Tues / Fri	July / July / July / July

1 How often / Amy brush / teeth?

How often does Amy brush her teeth?

She brushes her teeth three times a day.

2 How often / Emma / play video games?

3 How often / Louisa / visit her grandmother?

4 How often / Juan / go to school by bus?

5 How often / Chris late for school?

6 How often / Maria and Mario / take a vacation?

Use your English: Express surprise and comment

4 ★ **Number the conversation in the correct order.**

a) [ ] **Alfie:** A concert? Wow! That's great.

b) [ ] **Alfie:** I eat it every day.

c) [ ] **Alfie:** Once a year. I go swimming on vacation.

d) [ ] **Alfie:** Really? No TV? That's interesting. What do you do at night?

e) [ ] **Alfie:** Wow! That's great. And how often do you watch TV?

f) [ ] **Oliver:** Every day? You're joking! That's awful. How often do you exercise?

g) [1] **Oliver:** How often do you eat fast food?

h) [ ] **Oliver:** I play the piano. I'm in a concert next week.

i) [ ] **Oliver:** Never. We don't have a TV.

j) [11] **Oliver:** Thanks. Do you want to come to see me?

k) [ ] **Oliver:** Seriously? I exercise every day.

Consolidation

5 Look at the answers Mike has given to the survey and complete the sentences.

How often . . . ?

Do you have five minutes to complete our survey?

Your age: [14]   **Boy / Girl:** [B]   **Country:** [U.S.]

Click how often you do these things

Going out	Number of times	Time period
1 Go to the movies	1	week
2 Go to soccer games	2	month
3 Exercise or play sports	3	week
4 Hang out with family	8	month
Food		
5 Eat fast food	2	week
6 Eat fruit	3	day
7 Eat out	20	year
Study		
8 Do homework	every	day

1 He *goes* to the movies *once a week* .

2 He _____ to soccer games _____ .

3 He _____ or plays sports _____ .

4 He _____ with his family _____ .

5 He _____ fast food _____ .

6 He _____ fruit _____ .

7 He _____ out _____ .

8 He _____ homework _____ .

School days

INTEGRATED CONSOLIDATION SKILLS

Before you read

1 Before you read, check the meaning of these words.

New words
• sunny • jeans • meal

Read

2 ★ Read the three texts and say which country each fact relates to: Brazil (B), United States (US), or Finland (F).

Facts

1 School starts at 8 A.M. [B]

2 Breaks are half an hour. [ ]

3 There are lots of tests. [ ]

4 Students go to school six days a week. [ ]

5 Students get a hot lunch every day. [ ]

6 School finishes at 1 P.M. [ ]

7 There are ten-minute breaks. [ ]

Julia

Raul

Elena

Julia left a message for Raul and Elena.

1 Hi from sunny Brazil. School starts at 8 A.M. All classes are 45 minutes long. After each class, there's a break of five or ten minutes. Students don't wear a uniform, so I wear jeans. That's the ONLY good thing. Every week, we have lots of tests. School is over at one o'clock in the afternoon, but I do homework for two or three hours. I have some homework to do now, so see you later!

Raul left this message for Julia and Elena.

2 Hi there, Julia! Good luck with the homework. I'm at the International School in Los Angeles. My school day starts at eight thirty and ends at one thirty but . . . I go to school six days a week! We have classes on Saturdays! It's awful! I study English three days a week in the afternoons. Now I can talk about soccer with the boys in my class! How's your Portuguese???

Elena left this message for Julia and Raul.

3   Hello, you two. Good to hear your news. Finland's great, and this school is amazing. We start at eight o'clock, but it's OK because the classes are really interesting. There are 30-minute breaks. Students go outside for every break, even in the winter!! Sometimes it's −20°C here in January! School is over at two o'clock. I eat at school. Lunches are great. We have hot meals every day!

3 ★★ Read the texts again and answer the questions.

1 What time do classes start in Brazil?

At eight o'clock.

2 Do students wear uniforms at the school in Brazil?

_____

3 How often does Raul go to school?

_____

4 Does Raul study English in the afternoon?

_____

5 Does Elena bring her lunch to school?

_____

6 What time does Elena finish school?

_____

Listen

4 ★ 🎧 ⑦ Listen to the conversation between two students and complete the notes about England (E) and New Zealand (NZ).

1 School day starts: **E** *9:00 A.M.* **NZ** *8:30 A.M.*

2 School day ends: **E** _____ **NZ** _____

3 School year starts: **E** _____ **NZ** _____

4 Primary school ages: **E** 5–11 **NZ** _____

5 Intermediate school ages: **NZ** _____

6 Secondary school ages: **E** _____ **NZ** 13–17

Write

Writing tip: *and, but, because, so*

Remember! Use *and, but, because,* and *so* to combine two parts of a sentence.

*Guy leaves home at 8:15 **and** walks to school.*

*Some students pack a lunch, **but** Guy likes a hot meal.*

*On Wednesday, he has a quick lunch **because** he has Computer Club.*

*He's on the school soccer team **so** he often plays a game on Saturday.*

5 ★ Circle the correct endings for the sentences.

1 I get up early because . . .

a) school starts early.   b) I am very tired.

2 I don't play soccer at school because . . .

a) the breaks are short.   b) some people do.

3 I live in Italy so . . .

a) I don't speak Italian.   b) I go to an Italian school.

4 A lot of people eat school lunches, but . . .

a) I bring my lunch.   b) they are very good.

5 We don't have a school uniform, so . . .

a) we can't wear jeans.   b) we can wear jeans.

6 ★★ Complete the sentences with the correct endings from the box.

I don't wear sneakers
she goes to elementary school
she's very tall
~~we don't wear uniforms~~
we have 40 lessons a week

1 I wear jeans to school because *we don't*
wear uniforms _____ .

2 I wear jeans to school, but _____

_____ .

3 We have eight lessons a day, so _____

_____ .

4 My sister is seven, so _____

_____ .

5 My sister is seven, but _____

_____ .

Can you run five miles?

Vocabulary: Verbs of ability

1 ★ Circle the correct words.

1 (Play) / Do / Sing the guitar.

2 Take / Make / Use a washing machine.

3 Use / Work / Play a computer.

4 Draw / Ride / Make a picture.

5 Put / Sew / Make on a button.

6 Drive / Go / Ride a horse.

7 Do / Make / Take photographs.

8 Cook / Do / Use a meal.

2 ★★ Complete the ads for youth helpers with the words from the box.

- button • cake • computer • creative
- horse • instrument • photographs
- physical • pictures • ~~practical~~
- swim • tennis

---

1 _Practical_ **person needed**

- Can you sew on a 2 _____ ?
- Can you bake a 3 _____ ?
- Can you use a 4 _____ ?

We need young people to help at the Senior Center on weekends.

Tel: 415–555–0333

Active, sporty, 5 _____ **people wanted**

- Can you 6 _____ ?
- Can you ride a 7 _____ ?
- Can you play 8 _____ ?

We need you to help at our children's summer camp.

Email: summercamp@adventure.com

We want a 9 _____ **person for our summer community program.**

- Can you play a musical 10 _____ ?
- Can you paint or draw beautiful 11 _____ ?
- Can you take fantastic 12 _____ ?

Telephone: 805–555–4141

Grammar: Adverb: (not) very well
Can (present ability)

3 ★ Look at the pictures and complete the sentences with _can / very well_ or _can't / very well._

1 Sofia _can_ ride a horse _____ .

2 Sofia _____ play the guitar _____ .

3 Kelly _____ paint beautiful pictures _____ .

4 Kelly _____ cook dinner _____ .

5 Mr. Flores _____ use a washing machine _____ .

6 Mr. Flores _____ take photographs _____ .

7 Mrs. Flores _____ play soccer _____ .

8 Mrs. Flores _____ sew on a button _____ .

9 Jack and Emma _____ play tennis _____ .

10 Jack and Emma _____ dance _____ .

4 ★★ **Use the cues to ask and answer questions about the people in the pictures on page 50.**

1 Sofia / ride a horse?

Can Sofia ride a horse?

Yes, she can.

2 Sofia / play the guitar?

No, Sofia can't play the guitar very well.

_____

3 Kelly / paint nice pictures?

_____

_____

4 Kelly / cook dinner?

_____

_____

5 Mr. Flores / use a washing machine?

_____

_____

6 Mr. Flores / take good photographs?

_____

_____

7 Mrs. Flores / play soccer?

_____

_____

8 Mrs. Flores / sew on a button?

_____

_____

9 Jack and Emma / play tennis?

_____

_____

10 Jack and Emma / dance?

_____

_____

5 ★★ **Circle the correct words.**

Natalie: We want to put out a school magazine.

1 *You can / You can't /* (*Can you*) help?

Molly: I don't think so. 2 *I can't / Can I / I can* write very well.

Helen: 3 *You can / Can you / I can* take photographs?

Molly: Yes, 4 *I can take. / I can't. / I can.* 5 *I can't / Can I / I can* take photos to help.

Natalie: And I 6 *can't / can / can you* use a computer.

Molly: Hey, there's Leo and Sara. 7 *They can / Can they / Can* play the guitar very well.

Natalie: Molly! It's a magazine!

Molly: Yes, I know. We 8 *can / can't / can we* make a CD of it.

Helen: Hey, Molly, 9 *you can / can I / can you* cook?

Molly: No, 10 *I can / you can't / I can't.* Why? Do you want a food page in the magazine?

Consolidation

6 **Complete the text with the correct form of** *can* **and the verbs in parentheses.**

DID YOU KNOW . . . ?

Find out about the stars on Star Ability

Hey, did you know? George Clooney 1 *can play* (play) baseball very well. And he 2 _____ (draw) people, too. 3 _____ he _____ (sing)? Yes, he 4 _____ . And now he has a house in Italy on Lake Como so, 5 _____ he _____ (speak) Italian? No, he 6 _____ . Not very well.

What about Catherine Zeta-Jones? She's a great actress and she 7 _____ (sing and dance) as well. She's from Wales, so 8 _____ she _____ (speak) Welsh? No, she 9 _____ . She's Welsh, but she 10 _____ (not speak) Welsh.

Vocabulary: Food

1 ★ Complete the crossword puzzle with the names of the foods in the pictures. Then read down the shaded squares to find out what is for dinner.

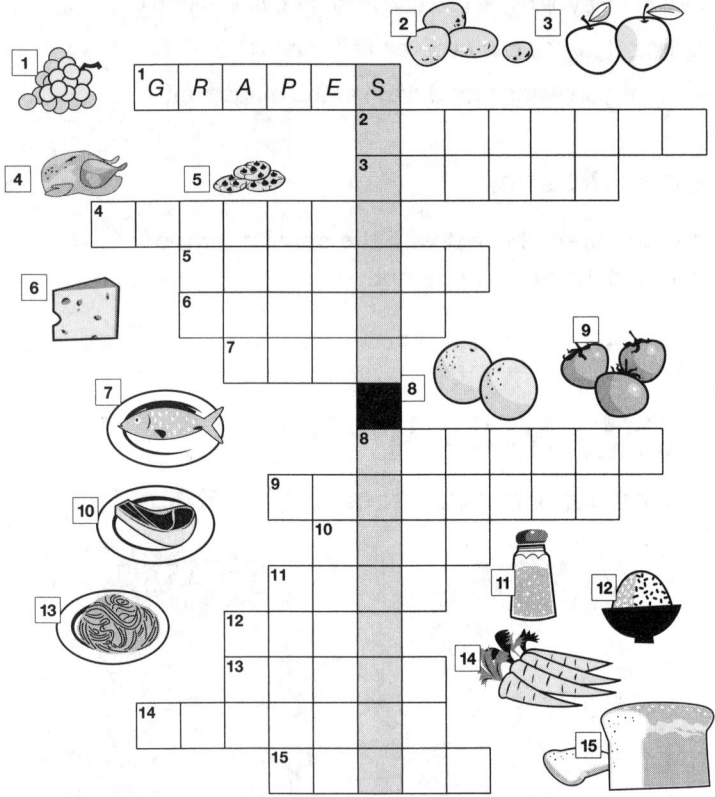

2 ★★ Unscramble the letters to make five more food items.

1 nnaaabs _bananas_   4 noosin _____

2 trebut _____   5 preepp _____

3 gesg _____   6 ragsu _____

Phrases

3 ★ Complete the conversations with the correct phrases from the box.

• here you are • I'm afraid • Not so fast.
• ~~What's the matter?~~

1 A: Oh no!

B: _What's the matter?_

A: I don't have any bread for my sandwiches.

2 A: Bye, Mom! See you later.

B: _____ You've got homework to do.

3 A: Do you have my apple?

B: Yes, _____ . It's in the bag.

4 A: _____ there's no dinner today. Sorry.

B: That's OK, I have sandwiches.

Grammar: Count and noncount nouns; *some* and *any*

4 ★ Circle the word which doesn't belong in each group (C = count, N = noncount).

1 **C** grapes cookies (cheese) apples

2 **C** potatoes meat oranges carrots

3 **N** apples butter chicken fruit

4 **C** tomatoes salt cookies eggs

5 **N** sugar fish bread bananas

6 **C** bananas pasta grapes onions

5 ★★ Write sentences about the kitchen.

1 (cheese) _There's some cheese._

2 (bananas?) _Are there any bananas?_
   Yes, there are.

3 (grapes) _____

4 (oranges?) _____

5 (meat) _____

6 (bread?) _____

7 (onions) _____

8 (sugar?) _____

Consolidation

6 Circle the correct answers.

Pizza ideas from around the world!

Close your eyes. Now think of a pizza. What can you see? **1** _____ onions? **2** _____ cheese? Of course, **3** _____ ! You can't have pizza without any cheese . . . can you? Yes, you can! In the U.S., **4** _____ chocolate pizzas! There isn't any **5** _____ , but **6** _____ white chocolate! In Japan, **7** _____ lots of pizzas with fish on them. The Japanese also eat pizza with egg and potatoes. Can you eat pizza and fast food? **8** _____ pizza with fast food on it? Yes, **9** _____ . **10** _____ a pizza with two cheeseburgers on it. Now, that is disgusting!

1 a) There is some   (b) Are there any   c) Is there any

2 a) Is there any   b) There are some   c) Are there any

3 a) there are   b) there is   c) there isn't

4 a) there is   b) is there   c) there are

5 a) onions   b) tomatoes   c) cheese

6 a) there are   b) there's   c) is there

7 a) there is   b) there are   c) there isn't

8 a) There is a   b) There are some   c) Is there a

9 a) there isn't   b) there is   c) there are

10 a) There's   b) Is there   c) There are

Extra challenge!

7 ★★★ Read the text, then draw and label the foods and drinks that are in the refrigerator.

There are some eggs. There's some cheese. There isn't any soda, but there's some orange juice. There are some carrots and some onions. There aren't any tomatoes, and there isn't any butter. There is some fish, but there isn't any chicken. There aren't any grapes, but there is an orange.

7c It's across from the bank.

Grammar: Imperatives

1 ★ **Match situations (1–8) with the imperatives (a–h).**

1 It's cold in here.
2 The last bus is at ten o'clock.
3 You don't understand?
4 Here's a CD.
5 Let's start the lesson.
6 Dad's asleep.
7 Have a good time in Spain.
8 I asked you a question.

a) Ask the teacher.
b) Listen to the second song.
c) Answer it now, please.
d) Call me!
e) Close the window.
f) Speak quietly.
g) Leave the party at nine fifty.
h) Open your books.

2 ★★ **Make the imperatives in Exercise 1 negative. Then match them to the new situations from the box.**

I can't hear you.
It's awful!
It's hot in here.
Text me.
~~Use your dictionary.~~
We are watching a video for today's lesson.
You can do it for homework.
You can get a taxi at 11.

a) *Don't ask* the teacher.
   Use your dictionary.

b) _____ to the second song.
   _____

c) _____ it now.
   _____

d) _____ me.
   _____

e) _____ the window.
   _____

f) _____ quietly.
   _____

g) _____ the party at nine fifty.
   _____

h) _____ your books.
   _____

Vocabulary: Places in town

3 ★ **Match the places (1–8) to the things you can do (a–h).**

Things to do in Smalltown!
You can go to the . . .

1 drugstore
2 bookstore
3 park
4 post office
5 restaurant
6 train station
7 supermarket
8 coffee shop

a) to get a cup of coffee.
b) to buy some stamps.
c) to eat lunch.
d) to get a train.
e) to get some medicine.
f) to get a new book.
g) to go for a walk.
h) to get some food for breakfast.

You can go somewhere else to have a good time!

4 ★★ **Complete the conversations with the correct places.**

1 A: Excuse me. I need some money.
   Where's the *bank*?
   B: I'm sorry. I don't know.

2 A: Let's have a cup of coffee.
   B: Oh yes. Is there a c_____
   s_____ here?

3 A: Where can we park?
   B: I don't know. Where's the p_____
   l_____ ?

4 A: Can I mail these letters?
   B: Yes. We can go to the p_____
   o_____ this afternoon.

5 A: I need some exercise.
   B: Let's go to the new h_____
   c_____ .

Grammar: Prepositions of place

5 ★ **Look at the map. Are the statements true (T) or false (F)? Correct the incorrect statements.**

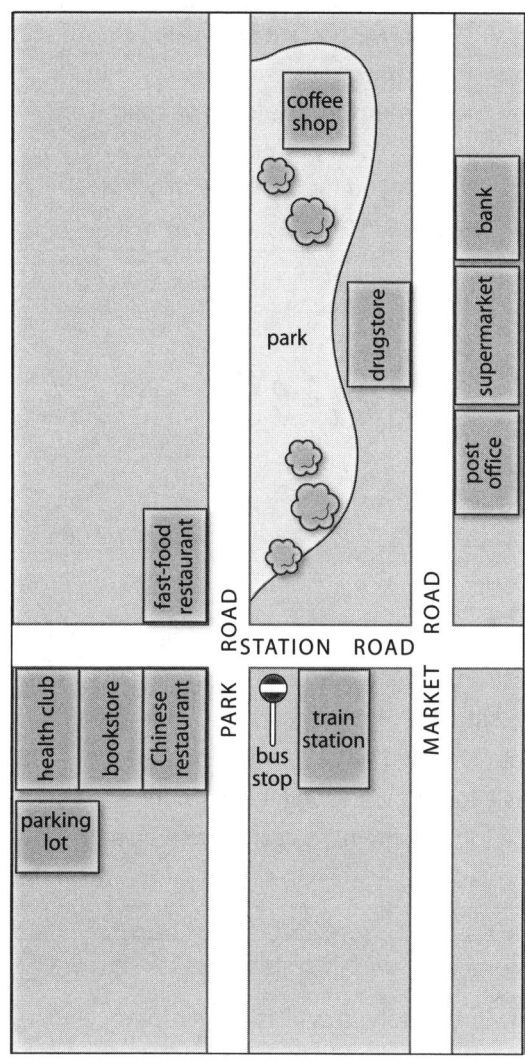

in
1 There's a coffee shop ~~across from~~ the park. ☐ *F*

2 There's a bus stop near the train station. ☐

3 There's a supermarket between the bank and the post office. ☐

4 There's a drugstore on the corner of Station Road and Market Road. ☐

5 The drugstore is next to the supermarket. ☐

6 The health club is next to the bookstore. ☐

7 The health club is in front of the parking lot. ☐

8 The train station is on Park Road. ☐

Use your English: Ask for help in town

6 ★ **Complete the conversations with words from the box.**

• between • ~~Excuse~~ • in • Is • know • near • next • opposite • sorry

1 **A:** *Excuse* me. Where's the health club?

   B: It's _____ Station Road, _____ to the bookstore.

2 **A:** Excuse me. _____ there a supermarket _____ here?

   B: Yes, there's one on Market Road, _____ the bank and the post office. It's _____ the drugstore.

3 **A:** Excuse me. Where's the mall?

   B: I'm _____ , I don't _____ .

Consolidation

7 **Circle the correct words.**

Camden Town

Camden Town is **1** *across from / (between) / behind* busy Kings Cross and beautiful Hampstead in North London. Camden is next **2** *to / from / of* Regent's Park. On a cold day, you can take a train, but when the sun is out and it's warm, **3** *walk you / to walk / walk*! The park is beautiful. **4** *Not / Don't / Doesn't* forget the London Zoo in the park. It's amazing!

There are some great markets **5** *next / near / between* the park. **6** *Don't you / You don't / Don't* come late because the markets close at about 4 P.M. **7** *Across from / Between / In front* one of the markets are the MTV studios. **8** *Come / You come / To come* here on a Friday and meet the MTV DJ Matt Willis! There's a fantastic sports arena **9** *in / at / on* the corner of Arlington Road and Parkway, and there are some great stores and coffee shops.

Next time you're in London, **10** *you visit / visit / do you visit* Camden Town!

Healthy or unhealthy diet?

Before you read

1 Before you read, check the meaning of these words.

New words
- calories • courses • cream • duck • popular
- sauce

Learning strategy: Focus your reading
Remember! Before you read, look at the comprehension task. This will help you focus on the information you need.

Healthy eating ideas
from around the world

Elena from Mexico says, "Eat more vegetables. You can eat some meat, but don't eat too much. In Mexico, we eat a lot of vegetables. Corn and beans are very popular. Meat has a lot of calories. Don't eat duck! It has a lot of fat. Eat vegetables, nuts, and fish. They have a lot of protein. You can have a balanced diet without any fat."

Fabio from Italy says, "Eat slowly. In my country, meals are a time to be with your family. It's fun to relax and talk. Health isn't only diet. You need a healthy lifestyle, too. Enjoy your meals. Have a ten-minute break between courses. Don't watch TV when you eat."

Kayo from Japan says, "Don't eat big meals. The French like cream and sauces, but their meals are only 75% the size of a meal in the U.S. We eat small dinners in Japan, too. In Okinawa, they say *Hara hachi bu*. It means 'eight parts out of ten.' "Stop eating when you are 80% full!"

Read

2 ★ Match the tips (1–5) with the countries they correspond to.

> **Tips**
>
> 1 Don't eat a lot of meat.
> *Mexico*
>
> 2 Don't eat quickly.
>
> _____
>
> 3 Don't eat a lot.
>
> _____
>
> 4 Eat meals with your family.
>
> _____
>
> 5 Eat vegetables, fish, and nuts.
>
> _____

3 ★★ Read the texts again and circle the correct endings.

1 In Mexico, they . . .
   a) don't eat meat.
   b) don't eat a lot of meat.
   c) eat a lot of meat.

2 Elena says, "Don't eat . . .
   a) fish."
   b) nuts."
   c) duck."

3 Italians often eat . . .
   a) in front of the TV.
   b) their dinner in ten minutes.
   c) with their families.

4 It's good to eat . . .
   a) quickly.
   b) slowly.
   c) a lot.

5 The Japanese eat . . .
   a) big meals.
   b) small meals.
   c) the same meals as Italians.

Listen

4 ★ 🎧 8 Listen to the conversation about unhealthy food and complete the names of the foods in the left-hand column of the chart.

Top five unhealthy foods

Name	Ingredients
1 _____ Benedict	*eggs,* _____ , _____
2 _____	_____ , _____ , _____
3 _____ confit	_____ , _____
4 _____	_____
5 _____ Alfredo	_____ , _____ , _____ , _____

5 ★★ 🎧 8 Listen again and write the ingredients in the right-hand column of the chart.

Write

6 ★ Look at the website. Write a similar answer in your notebook about what you eat using the cues below.

Healthy or unhealthy? What do you eat?

Ernesto, Fresno, California

Am I healthy or unhealthy? I don't know. I eat some healthy food. I always have orange juice for breakfast. I have cheese sandwiches, a carrot, and an apple for lunch, and I usually have meat and vegetables for dinner.

I eat unhealthy food, too. I often have potato chips at school and sometimes I buy chocolate. I drink soda about three times a week, and I eat pizza every Friday night.

- I eat some healthy food.
- I _____ for breakfast.
- For lunch, I . . .
- At night, I . . .
- I eat unhealthy food, too.
- I love . . .
- On the weekend, I sometimes eat _____ and on vacation, I always . . .

What's he doing in California?

Phrases

1 ★ **Circle the correct words.**

Mom: Antonio!

Antonio: Hang **1** *(on)* / *up* / *out* a minute, Mom! I'm on the phone . . . Yes?

Mom: Where's Alicia?

Antonio: She's not here. Believe it or **2** *no* / *don't* / *not*, she's swimming.

Mom: In this weather?

Antonio: Yes. Why, what's wrong?

Mom: It's Dad's concert today. He's expecting us.

Antonio: Oh no! There's a big soccer game on TV.

Mom: Sorry. It's Dad's big day, too. Come **3** *on* / *out* / *in*! Hurry up.

Antonio: But Alicia's not here.

Mom: Bring the video camera and tape the concert. Alicia can watch it later.

Antonio: How **4** *warm* / *cool* / *awful*! What a great idea, Mom!

Grammar: Present continuous

2 ★ **Look at the picture. Complete the sentences with the verbs in parentheses in the correct form.**

1 Jake is *texting. He isn't sleeping*

_____ .

(text / sleep)

2 Kim _____

_____ .

(drink / eat)

3 Lucas _____

_____ .

(write / look out of the window)

4 Laura and Beth _____

_____ .

(talk / read)

5 Esteban _____

_____ .

(use a laptop / text)

6 Mia _____

_____

_____ .

(listen to an MP3 player / text)

Free time

8

3 ★★ **Complete the phone conversation with the correct form of verbs from the box.**

> • do • do • do • help • make • sit
> • wait • watch • watch

Camila: Hi, Luz.

Luz: Hi Camila. What **1** *are* you *doing*?

Camila: I **2** _____ in my bedroom.

Luz: **3** _____ you _____
Avatar again?

Camila: No, I'm not. My brother **4** _____
that. I have the *Shrek 3* DVD.

Luz: Really? Can I watch it?

Camila: Of course. What **5** _____ you _____
now?

Luz: I **6** _____ my mom.
We **7** _____ a cake.

Camila: Oh wow! Sorry.

Luz: Don't worry. We **8** _____
anything now. The cake's in the oven. We
9 _____ for it to be done.

Camila: Well, come over and watch *Shrek* later, and
bring me some cake.

Luz: Sure. No problem!

Vocabulary: The weather

4 ★ **Match the words from the box with the correct symbols.**

> • cloudy • foggy • raining
> • snowing • sunny • windy

1 It's *raining*

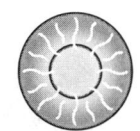
2 It's _____

3 It's _____

4 It's _____

5 It's _____

6 It's _____

Consolidation

5 **Look at pictures A and B and find five more differences between them.**

Picture A

Picture B

1 In picture A, *it's sunny / the sun is shining*, but in
picture B, *it's cloudy*.

2 In picture A, _____ ,
but in picture B, _____ .

3 _____
_____
_____

4 _____
_____
_____

5 _____
_____
_____

6 _____
_____

Vocabulary: Sports

1 ★ **Complete the sports words with the missing vowels.**

1 s_cc_r

2 _thl_t_

3 t_nn_s

4 b_sk_tb_ll

5 sw_mm_ng

6 g_mn_st_cs

2 ★ **Write each sport from the box in the correct category.**

| • ~~basketball~~ • soccer • swimming |
| • tennis • volleyball • windsurfing |

• **With a ball:** _basketball_ , _____ , _____ , _____

• **On / in water:** _____ , _____

Grammar: Simple present and present continuous

3 ★ **Read about soccer and circle the correct form of the verbs.**

Crazy about soccer . . .

How popular is soccer? Research shows that about three quarters of young people your age in Latin America watch soccer on TV regularly. And you probably know that more and more young people around the world are **1** *play* /*playing* the game. So exactly who plays soccer? As for the professionals, it's not just men, but women who play. There are even all-women teams. And many of these women are soccer stars! Just ask Faye White. She's the captain of the women's soccer team in England. In this photo, she's **2** *hold* / *holding* up a prize cup!

And while on the subject of prize cups, nearly every four years since 1930, the World Cup takes place. These days, you'll find people everywhere who are **3** *watch* / *watching* this amazing soccer competition. Everyone has a favorite player or team. Names like Ronaldo and David Beckham **4** *become* / *are becoming* ones that almost everyone recognizes. The Brazilian team went to every tournament and won the cup five times! In fact, Brazil is already **5** *prepares* / *preparing* to host the World Cup in 2014. Even years before the big event, people **6** *work* / *are working* hard to get Mineirao Stadium ready for the record crowds.

4 ★★ Write questions in the simple present or present continuous using the cues. Answer them according to the information in the article.

1 How often / World Cup / occur?

How often does the World Cup occur?

It occurs every four years.

2 What / more and more young people / do?

_____

_____

3 What / kind of team / Faye / play on?

_____

_____

_____

4 What / Faye / hold up / in the photo?

_____

_____

_____

5 Who / watch / World Cup?

_____

_____

_____

6 Which names / become / recognized by every one?

_____

_____

_____

7 Which country / prepare to host / 2014 World Cup?

_____

_____

_____

5 ★★ Complete the conversations with the correct form of the verbs.

go

Meg: Hello, where **1** *are you going?*

Dan: I **2** _____ to the music room.

Meg: Why?

Dan: I always **3** _____ to the music room at lunchtime.

do

Mom: **4** _____ your homework now?

Liam: No, I'm not.

Mom: But you always **5** _____ your homework in the afternoon.

Liam: Yes, but I **6** _____ it now because we don't have any today!

play

Sara: What game **7** _____ now?

Joe: It's a new video game. Do you play video games?

Sara: No, I don't. I never **8** _____ video games, but my brother **9** _____ them all the time.

Consolidation

6 Complete the conversation with the correct form of words from the box.

┌───┐
│ • do • go • go • not go • play • play • rain │
│ • team • volleyball   │
└───┘

Mike: Where's Rob?

Leo: He's outside.

Mike: What **1** *'s* he *doing*?

Leo: He **2** _____ soccer.

Mike: He hates soccer. He never plays **3** _____ sports.

Leo: I know. He usually **4** _____ swimming on Thursday mornings, but the pool is closed today, so they **5** _____ outside.

Mike: But it **6** _____ ! Students **7** _____ usually _____ outside when it rains. They play indoor sports like basketball or **8** _____ .

Leo: Where **9** _____ you _____?

Mike: To the library.

Leo: Do you need a book?

Mike: No. You can see the sports field from there. I want to see Rob playing soccer in the rain!

8c I prefer being outside.

Vocabulary: Free-time activities

1 ★ **Look at the pictures and complete the activities with *have*, *go*, or *go to*.**

1 *go* swimming   4 _____ a concert
2 _____ the beach   5 _____ jogging
3 _____ a barbecue   6 _____ a party

2 ★★ **Complete the sentences with the correct verbs.**

1 Cell phone calls are expensive, so I *chat* online with my friends instead.
2 There's nothing good on TV, so let's w_____ a DVD.
3 Paul can't hear the phone because he's l_____ to a CD in his bedroom.

4 I want to play the guitar well, so I p_____ every day.
5 At night, I usually s_____ the net looking for good games to play.

Grammar: *Like, love, hate, prefer + -ing*

3 ★ **Look at the symbols and write sentences.**

😍 = love 😊 = like 🙁 = don't like 😫 = hate

1 I 🙁 jogging.
   I don't like jogging.
2 My brother 😍 surfing the net.
   _____
3 My friends 😊 shopping.
   _____
4 My sister 😫 watching DVDs.
   _____
5 I 😍 reading.
   _____
6 My parents 🙁 having barbecues.
   _____

4 ★★ **Complete the sentences with the correct form of the verbs in parentheses.**

1 I *love chatting* (love / chat) with my friends online.
2 My mother _____ (like / jog).
3 My friends _____ (prefer / go) swimming to _____ (go) to the movies.
4 _____ you _____ (like / play) volleyball?
5 I really _____ (hate / go) shopping with my parents.
6 We _____ (not like / watch) TV.
7 _____ you _____ (prefer / have) barbecues or _____ (go) out to eat?

Use your English: Make and respond to suggestions

5 ★ Complete the conversation with phrases from the box. Circle the correct answers.

a) about going	e) Let's go
b) don't you do	f) Let's have it
c) great idea	g) not sure
d) How about having	h) not today

Brett: Hi Antonio! **1** _____ a party on Saturday?

Antonio: I'm **2** _____ . Where?

Brett: **3** _____ here.

Antonio: That's a **4** _____ . Ernie? What do you think?

Ernie: Sorry. What?

Antonio: A party.

Ernie: No, **5** _____ . I've got a lot of homework.

Antonio: No. On Saturday.

Ernie: Oh, OK.

Antonio: So what about now? Do you want to do something?

Ernie: No. I'm busy.

Antonio: Why **6** _____ that tonight?

Brett: Yes. Come on, big brother! **7** _____ out.

Ernie: Where?

Antonio: What **8** _____ shopping?

Ernie: Yeah. OK. I can buy a new CD.

Consolidation

6 Complete the text with words from the box.

• about • being • do • don't
• going • prefer • to • watching

What kind of a person are you?

Outdoor people 1 _prefer_ playing sports to playing video games.

They prefer windsurfing **2** _____ surfing the net.

Outdoor people love **3** _____ outside, whether it's nice out or not.

Indoor people prefer **4** _____ TV in their bedrooms to watching people outside.

They like **5** _____ shopping online, not at the mall.

Are you an indoor person? Where **6** _____ you prefer meeting your friends? Online or outside?

Why **7** _____ you do something different?

How **8** _____ trying a sport or going for a walk? It's good for you and it's fun.

Extra challenge!

7 ★★★ Are you an indoor or outdoor person?

a) Write your own sentences about the activities from the box using *love / like / don't like / hate*.

• going out • jogging • watching TV
• playing video games • swimming

I hate jogging. _____

b) Write your own sentences about the pairs of activities from the box, saying which you prefer.

• watching TV / going to the movies
• hanging out / chatting online

I prefer watching TV to going to the movies. ___

Values for living
School blog

INTEGRATED
CONSOLIDATION
SKILLS

Before you read

1 Before you read, check the meaning of these words.

> **New words**
> • post (a message) • blog • drive (me) crazy

HOME | **BLOGS** | GROUPS | VIDEO | CHAT

West Green School **Blog site**

Topics	Posts	Last post by	Time of post
What are you doing?	34	Emily	Mon 5/10 7:56 P.M.
Likes and dislikes	21	Emily	Mon 5/10 8:13 P.M.
Boys and girls	51	Emily	Mon 5/10 8:28 P.M.
School work	147	Emily	Mon 5/10 8:45 P.M.

1 Topic: What are you doing?
Post: Emily
I'm in my bedroom. My parents think I'm studying, but I'm not. I'm reading all the posts on this site. They're great. I'm listening to music on my MP3 player.

2 Topic: Boys and girls
Post: Emily
I'm going out with Manuel on his birthday. I'm looking at a photo of him now. We usually see each other on Saturday afternoons at soccer games. He doesn't like shopping, but he loves going to the Mexican restaurant at the mall. Wow! He's so cool.

3 Topic: Likes and dislikes
Post: Emily
I love listening to music, watching DVDs, surfing the net, playing basketball, texting, and sleeping. I don't like getting up, doing homework, helping around the house, or reading.

4 Topic: Schoolwork
Post: Emily
We have exams soon. I don't like studying for exams. I don't like doing my homework. I'm 13 and I want to have a good time! What do I do? IT'S DRIVING ME CRAZY!!!

Read

2 ★ **Look at the four posts on the school blog and answer the questions.**

1 Where is Emily?

She's in her bedroom.

2 What is she doing?

_____

3 What is she listening to on her MP3 player?

_____

4 What is she looking at?

_____

5 Does she like playing basketball?

_____

6 Does she like reading?

_____

7 Where does Manuel like going?

_____

8 Does Emily like studying?

_____

Listen

Learning strategy: Use pictures to predict
Remember! Before you listen, look at the picture that goes with the text. Pictures can give you clues about the subject matter of the text.

3 ★ **Before you listen, look at the pictures below and the posts on the blog. Can you predict what you are going to hear? Circle the correct answers.**

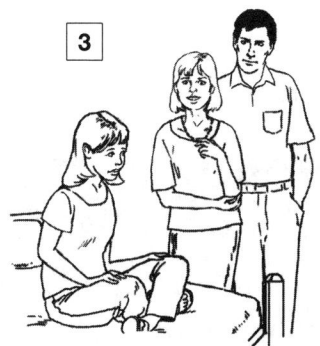

1 What is Emily doing when the woman comes into the room?
  a) Doing her homework
  b) Using her computer
  c) Talking to a friend on the phone

2 What is the woman reading in picture 2?
  a) The blog
  b) A letter
  c) A book

3 Who do you think the people in picture 3 are?
  a) Emily, her mother, and a friend
  b) Emily and her parents
  c) Emily and her brother and sister

4 What do you think the man and woman are talking to Emily about?
  a) Her birthday
  b) Her schoolwork
  c) Their vacation

4 ★ 🎧 9 **Listen to the conversation and check your answers to Exercise 3.**

5 ★★ 🎧 9 **Listen again. Are the sentences true (T) or false (F)?**

1 Emily's mother has dinner for Emily. `F`

2 Emily says she is taking a break from her studying. ☐

3 Emily's mom reads Emily's posts on the blog. ☐

4 Emily's father is not at home. ☐

5 Emily's parents say that she can't use her computer again. ☐

6 Emily's parents don't want Emily to go out with Manuel. ☐

Write

6 ★ **Write your own posts for two of the topics in your notebook. Use Emily's posts to help you.**

Vocabulary: Past adverbial expressions: *yesterday*, *last year/night*

1 ★ **Replace the underlined phrases with a phrase from the box that has the same meaning.**

• last month • last night • last Wednesday • last week • last weekend • last year • this morning • ~~yesterday~~

1 I was at the movies <u>on September 4 in the afternoon</u>. *(It is now September 5.)*
   I was at the movies *yesterday*.

2 I was on vacation <u>in March</u>. *(It is now April.)*
   I was on vacation _____ .

3 I was at the Youth Club <u>on Wednesday, the 20th of July</u>. *(It is now Monday, the 25th of July.)*
   I was at the Youth Club _____ .

4 I was at my grandmother's house <u>on Saturday, the 10th and Sunday, the 11th of May</u>. *(It is now the 18th of May.)*
   I was at my grandmother's house _____
   _____ .

5 I was in the eighth grade <u>from September 2007 to June 2008</u>. *(It is now September 2008.)*
   I was in the eighth grade _____
   _____ .

6 I was in an English class <u>today at 10 A.M.</u> *(It is now 2 P.M.)*
   I was in an English class _____
   _____ .

7 I was at the movies <u>on Wednesday, the 15th of August and Friday, the 17th of August</u>. *(It's now Friday, the 24th of August.)*
   I was at the movies twice _____
   _____ .

8 My father was at work <u>from 6 P.M. yesterday to 11:30 P.M.</u> *(It is now 2 P.M. the next day.)*
   My father was at work _____ .

Grammar: Simple past of *be*

2 ★ **Complete the text with the correct form of *be* (+ affirmative or – negative).**

Name: Josh Barnes
Date: June 13th

🏛 **METROPOLITAN POLICE**

Statement

At four o'clock on Saturday, the 9th of June, I **1** <u>*was*</u> (+) at the mall with my friends. We **2** _____ (+) there for an hour. My cell phone **3** _____ (+) in my bag. We **4** _____ (+) in one of the restaurants in the food court downstairs. We **5** _____ (–) in any stores. My bag **6** _____ (–) open. It **7** _____ (+) closed all the time. At six o'clock, I **8** _____ back (+) at home, but my phone **9** _____ (–) in my bag.

3 ★★ Write sentences about the events on the calendar using the cues.
Use the correct form of the verb *be* and a past adverbial phrase.

APRIL

Mon		**1**
Tues	me/movies	**2**
Wed		**3**
Thurs	Mom and Dad/ movies	**4**
Fri		**5**
Sat	me + Sara at Grandma's	**6**
Sun		**7**

afternoon—me/ my friend's house	**8**
night—Leo and Will on TV	
A.M. my class/ concert	**9**
	TODAY

1 I / the movies / Tuesday

   I was at the movies last Tuesday.

2 Mom and Dad / the movies / Wednesday

   _____

   _____

3 Sara and I / our grandmother's house / weekend

   _____

   _____

4 I / at my friend's house / yesterday

   _____

   _____

5 Leo and Will / on TV / last night

   _____

   _____

6 My class / at a concert / morning

   _____

   _____

Consolidation

4 Complete the text with words from the box.

• last • last night • That's
• The next • ~~was~~ • was • wasn't
• were • weren't • weren't

The Lost Boys in concert

I **1** *was* at The Lost Boys concert **2** _____ night. They were tired, so they **3** _____ very good. **4** _____ because this was their 15th concert in 14 days. On their first night, they **5** _____ fantastic, but the concert **6** _____ was very different. It **7** _____ a good night for the band. Singer Billy Davies and guitarist Sam Fisher **8** _____ happy. But don't worry. It's not the end of The Lost Boys. **9** _____ morning, the band **10** _____ on a plane back home to the U.S. for a two-month break and next week, their great new CD is out!

She climbed up a crane!

Grammar: Simple past of regular verbs: affirmative and negative

1 ★ Read the story and write the verbs in parentheses in the simple past.

It was a dark, cold, rainy night; and we were lost. Suddenly, we **1** _noticed_ (notice) an old house. We **2** _____ (walk) up to the big, old door; and Dan **3** _____ (knock). The door **4** _____ (open), but there wasn't anybody there. I **5** _____ (want) to leave, but we **6** _____ (wait) and we **7** _____ (listen). After five minutes, we decided to go in. The door **8** _____ (close) with a loud BANG!

2 ★★ Read the second part of the story and then complete the sentences to correct the mistakes.

Kelly tried to open the door. "I can't!" she cried. We waited for five long minutes and then climbed up the stairs. We looked in all the rooms. There was nothing. Suddenly, we stopped. There, in front of us, was a very short man with long gray hair. "What do you want?" he asked. Dan answered, "We were lost, we wanted a place to sleep. We . . ." He stopped. We looked up and suddenly realized what was wrong. The man wasn't there . . .

1 Dan tried to open the door.
Dan _didn't try_ to open the door. _Kelly tried_ to open the door.

2 They waited for ten minutes.
They _____ for ten minutes. They _____ minutes.

3 They climbed down the stairs.
They _____ down the stairs.
They _____ the stairs.

4 They looked through the windows.
They _____ through the windows.
They _____ all the rooms.

5 A woman asked "What do you want?"
A woman _____ "What do you want?"
A _____ "What do you want?"

6 Kelly answered the man.
Kelly _____ the man.
_____ the man.

Grammar: Prepositions of motion

3 ★ Label the picture on the next page with words from the box.

- across • along • down • into
- out of • past • ~~up~~

Consolidation

4 Read the blog about some crazy dreams. Some verbs and prepositions are missing. Complete the blog with words from each box. Use the correct form of the verbs in the affirmative or negative.

• answer • arrive
• ask • ~~call~~ • call
• did see • did think
• live • look • look
• notice • start
• walk • want

• across • down
• down • out of
• up • up

MY CRAZY DREAM . . .

I **1** _called_ a woman on my cell phone—a woman who **2** l_____ in the 1800s. She
3 a_____ my cell-phone call on _her_ cell! I **4** d_____ it was strange at all. She
5 s_____ to tell me about how she didn't **6** w_____ fish for dinner. Just then,
my mother **7** c_____ me to come **8** d_____ for late a dinner. And it was fish!

—Megan, age 14

My family and I **9** a_____ at our hotel for our summer vacation. We **10** n_____
that there were no people at the hotel—just us. We **11** w_____ **12** u_____ to the front
desk and **13** a_____ for a key to our room. The clerk said the rooms were all full. We **14** l_____
15 u_____ and **16** d_____ the halls. We **17** d_____ any other people! We **18** l_____
19 o_____ the window and **20** a_____ the street. There were no people in the whole town!

—Julio, age 13

Extra challenge!

5 ★★★ Write the end of the story about Kelly and Dan in your notebook. Use these verbs and prepositions of motion to help you.

• arrive • call • carry
• notice • open
• realize • wait • walk

• across • along
• down • into
• out of • past • up

Grammar: Simple past of regular verbs: questions, answers, and short answers

1 ★ Match the questions (1–8) to the answers (a–h).

1 Did you watch TV last night?
2 Did your brother pass his exams?
3 What did your father watch last night?
4 What game did you and your friends play?
5 Did your mother listen to her new CD?
6 Who did you talk to last night?
7 When did they finish their homework?
8 Did your friends surf the Internet last night?

a) We played *Tomb Raider*.
b) I talked to Mia on my cell phone.
c) Yes, I did.
d) No, they didn't.
e) They finished it at nine o'clock.
f) Yes, he did.
g) No, she didn't.
h) He watched a new movie on TV.

2 ★★ Read the article and complete the questions, short answers, and statements.

She can dance, sing, and act

Natalie Imbruglia is from Australia, but her father was Italian. He moved to Australia from Sicily. Natalie has three sisters. When they were young, the family lived near Sydney, and Natalie studied dancing. She started her acting career on TV in the show *Neighbours* when she was 16. Kylie Minogue also acted in *Neighbours*, but they didn't act together. After two years, Natalie moved to London and she started singing. Her first song, *Torn*, stayed at number one in England for 11 weeks. She also played Lorna Campbell in the film *Johnny English* with Rowan Atkinson (Mr. Bean).

She's amazing! Yesterday, we talked to her and asked her some questions . . .

1 *Did* Natalie's father *move* (move) to Canada?
(✗) *No, he didn't.* (Australia) *He moved to Australia.*

2 _____ Natalie's family _____ (live) in Brisbane?
(✗) _____ (near Sydney) _____
_____

3 _____ Natalie _____ (study) dancing when she was a child?
(✓) _____

4 _____ Natalie and Kylie _____ (act) together in *Neighbours*?
(✗) _____

5 _____ Natalie _____ (move) to the U.S.?
(✗) _____ (England) _____

6 _____ *Torn* _____ (stay) at number one in England for 12 weeks?
(✗) _____ (11 weeks) _____

7 _____ Natalie and Rowan Atkinson _____ (act) in the film *Johnny English*?
(✓) _____

Vocabulary: Adjectives of feeling

3 ★ Cross out the LEAST likely reason for each of Ben's feelings.

1 I'm worried.

  a) I have an important exam tomorrow.

  b) I can't find my cell phone.

  c) ~~It's my birthday tomorrow.~~

2 I'm happy.

  a) I'm on the school soccer team.

  b) Summer vacation starts tomorrow.

  c) It's raining, and I'm late for school.

3 I'm upset.

  a) I passed my English exam yesterday.

  b) My brother can go out at night, but I can't.

  c) My friends are going to the movies, but they didn't ask me.

4 I'm bored.

  a) There's nothing good on TV tonight.

  b) I have a new video game.

  c) It's raining, and there's nothing to do.

5 I'm angry.

  a) My friends are late, and the movie starts at five.

  b) My friends texted me last night.

  c) My best friend didn't remember my birthday.

6 I'm tired.

  a) I played video games until 4 A.M.

  b) We arrived home from vacation at three in the morning.

  c) I failed my science exam.

7 I'm sad.

  a) I played tennis yesterday.

  b) My best friend moved to Uruguay last week.

  c) The girl I like has a new boyfriend.

Use your English: Ask about problems

4 ★ Complete the conversation with phrases from the box.

> • Because • fine
> • just a little upset
> • Nothing
> • wrong
> • ~~What's the matter~~
> • Why don't you

A: Hi, Jamie.

B: Hello.

A: Oh, man. **1** _What's the matter_?

B: Nothing. I'm **2** _____ .

A: No, you aren't. What's **3** _____?

B: **4** _____ .

A: Jamie. Talk to me.

B: I'm **5** _____ .

A: Why?

B: **6** _____ I failed my English exam.

A: **7** _____ take it again?

B: That's a good idea!

Consolidation

5 Write questions and answers.

1 Lucas / be / bored last night? (✓)

  Was Lucas bored last night?

  Yes, he was.

2 he / watch / TV? (✓ Pop Idol)

  _____

  _____

3 he / like / it? (✗)

  _____

  _____

4 Lucas / be / happy this morning? (✗)

  _____

  _____

5 he / get to / school late? (✓)

  _____

  _____

Across cultures
Phones and flights

INTEGRATED CONSOLIDATION SKILLS

Before you read

1 Before you read, check the meaning of these words.

> **New words**
> • die (died) • mine *(n)* • create (created)
> • abroad • repair (repaired) • collections

Read

2 ★ Skim the text and put the events in the order they happened.

a) He worked abroad.

b) He created his first phone.

c) His father died. `1`

d) He started his own company.

e) He moved to Stockholm.

f) He returned to Sweden.

Who was Lars Ericsson?

Today, you may think of Bluetooth® when you hear the name Ericsson. But do you know about Lars Ericsson? Lars Magnus Ericsson was born in Sweden in 1846. His father died when he was 12. Lars then worked in a mine to help his family. In 1867, he moved to Stockholm. He worked for six years for a company, Ollers and Co. After that, he worked abroad from 1872 to 1875. He returned to Sweden in 1875, and he started his own telephone company with a friend. They repaired phones. Ericsson copied ideas from other phone companies like Bell and Siemens. In 1879, he created his own phone. Later, other companies copied *his* ideas. His work was very good, and his early phones are beautiful. Today, lots of people collect old phones; and they want to find early Ericsson phones for their collections.

3 ★★ Read the text again and answer the questions.

1 When was Lars Magnus Ericsson born?

   He was born in 1846.

2 How old was he when his father died?

_____

3 Where did he work when he was 12?

_____

4 When did he move to Stockholm?

_____

5 Who did he work for?

_____

6 How long did he work abroad?

_____

7 Who did Ericsson copy ideas from?

_____

8 When did he create his first phone?

_____

Listen

4 ★ 🎧 10 Listen to the conversation and circle the correct endings for the sentences.

1 Lucy is going on vacation with . . .

   a) her dad.

   b) her friend.

   c) her grandmother.

2 Who was worried about who and when?

   a) Lucy was worried about her grandmother.

   b) Lucy's father was worried about Lucy.

   c) In 1985, Lucy's grandmother was worried about Lucy's father.

5 ★★ (10) **Listen again and complete the sentences.**

1 Lucy's father was on vacation in *1985*.

2 His parents were very _____ about him.

3 He didn't call because the phone in the village

_____ .

4 Lucy's father missed the _____ home.

5 Lucy has an _____ on her cell phone.

6 Lucy's father didn't write because there wasn't a

_____ in the village.

7 Lucy's father moved to a different _____ .

8 Lucy is very _____ about her vacation.

> **Learning strategy: Review your work**
> **Remember!** Check your work carefully before you hand it in to your teacher. Read it two or three times: The first time, check the **grammar** and **vocabulary**; the second time, check the **spelling**; the third time, check the **punctuation**.

Write

6 ★ **Each sentence of the text has <u>one</u> mistake. Write the underlined word correctly.**

1 Did Alexander Graham Bell really <u>invented</u> the telephone?	*invent*
2 Some people say it was Elisha Grey. He was born in the <u>us</u> in 1835.	_____
3 Grey <u>works</u> on many important telegraph inventions before 1876.	_____
4 On the <u>fourteen</u> of February, 1876, Bell invented the telephone.	_____
5 But Grey also had a telephone invention and <u>wonted</u> to tell the world about his phone on the same day!	_____
6 Bell was first to tell the world, but some people think that he copied <u>Greys</u> ideas.	_____
7 No one really knows, but it is Bell that we <u>remmember</u> today.	_____

7 ★★ **Write a paragraph in your notebook about the world's first passenger jet airliner, using the notes and ideas below. Use Exercise 5 on page 83 of the Student Book to help you. Start like this:**

The first passenger jet airliner flight was on May 2nd, 1952.

- be – when?
- travel – where from / to?
- travel – how far?
- travel – how fast?
- last – how long? / then
- last – how long? / now

Name: De Havilland Comet 1
First flight: May 2, 1952
From: London
To: Johannesburg, South Africa
Speed: 497 mph
Distance: 6,835 miles
Flying time: 23 hours 40 minutes (five stops)
Flying time now: 12 hours (no stops)

Grammar: Simple past of irregular verbs: affirmative and negative

1 ★ Circle the correct words.

1 I *have* / *had* a good time yesterday.

2 Paulo *goes* / *went* to the movies on Saturday.

3 I *thought* / *think* my brother was late, but he wasn't.

4 Anna *got* / *get* to her hotel late last night.

5 My parents *drive* / *drove* to work yesterday.

6 Last week, this CD player *cost* / *costs* $75. Today, it's $100.

7 We *take* / *took* a taxi to the hotel yesterday.

8 We *bring* / *brought* our cameras to school last week.

2 ★ Make the sentences negative.

1 My cousin had 20 texts yesterday.

   My cousin *didn't have* 20 texts yesterday.

2 You saw three shows last night.

   You _____ three shows last night.

3 You paid $50 for your bus tickets.

   You _____ $50 for your bus tickets.

4 Our taxi driver drove very slowly.

   Our taxi driver _____ very slowly.

5 Ed took a photo of our class.

   Ed _____ a photo of our class.

6 They brought a cake to the party.

   They _____ a cake to the party.

7 My friend got a new cell phone last weekend.

   My friend _____ a new cell phone last weekend.

8 Paulo and Yoko went to Rio last summer.

   Paulo and Yoko _____ to Rio last summer.

3 ★★ Use correct form of the verbs in parentheses.

Fernando Alonso

Fernando Alonso was born in Spain in 1981. When Fernando and his sister, Lorena, were young, their father, José, 1 *drove* (drive) go-karts. He wasn't rich, but he wanted to give his daughter, Lorena, a go-kart. José 2 _____ (not buy) a go-kart because they 3 _____ (cost) a lot of money. He 4 _____ (make) one, and he 5 _____ (give) it to Lorena when she was eight years old. She didn't like karting, so Fernando 6 _____ (take) the kart. He was only three!

Fernando was a great young driver and moved from karting to race-car driving in his teens. He 7 _____ (come) in first in the Spanish junior championships four times. He 8 _____ (drive) in his first Formula 1 race in 2001 for Minardi.

In 2005 and 2006, Alonso 9 _____ (win) the F1 championship with Lotus; but he 10 _____ (not drive) for them in 2007. He moved to McLaren, but wasn't happy there and he 11 _____ (not win) a third championship.

4 ★★ **Read the article in Exercise 3 again and correct the sentences.**

1 Fernando Alonso's father drove Formula 1 cars.

Fernando Alonso's father didn't drive Formula 1
cars. He drove go-karts.

2 His father bought a go-kart.

_____

_____

3 Fernando's father made the kart for Fernando.

_____

_____

4 Fernando came in first in the Spanish junior
championships five times.

_____

_____

5 Fernando had his first Formula 1 race in 2002.

_____

_____

6 Fernando won the F1 Championship in 2007.

_____

_____

Vocabulary: Transportation

5 ★ **Label the types of transportation.**

1 p_lane_   2 b_____   3 c_____

4 t_____   5 m_____   6 b_____

7 t_____   8 b_____   9 t_____

Consolidation

6 **Complete the text with the correct form of
the words from the box.**

> • bike • by • go • ~~have~~ • not buy
> • not see • see • take • train

Gemma: Hi, Martha! I'm back from
New England. We **1** _had_ a great time.

Martha: Where . . . ?

Gemma: We flew to Boston **2** _____ plane. It
was cool. I **3** _____ The Freedom Trail
and we traveled by **4** _____.
Then we **5** _____ to Cambridge on the
6 _____ . I **7** _____ lots of photos, but
I **8** _____ the Red Sox play.

Martha: Why not . . . ?

Gemma: It wasn't baseball season!
I **9** _____ you a present.
Sorry.

Phrases

1 ★ **Complete the phrases.**

1 A: Did you eat any fast food in Spain?

   B: N_____ w_____ ! We ate good, local Spanish food.

2 A: W_____ b_____ from your trip!

   B: Thanks. It's great to be home.

3 The trip was t_____ a_____ . We sang all the way.

4 A: Here you are. A present from our vacation in Mexico.

   B: Oh, thank you very much. W_____ a m_____! This isn't from Mexico!

Vocabulary: Vacation activities

2 ★ **Label the pictures with activities from the box.**

- go climbing • go mountain biking
- go shopping • go sightseeing • go skiing
- go to a museum • go to the beach
- go windsurfing • sunbathe • swim
- play volleyball

Come to sunny Cape Cod

4 _____

5 _____

6 _____

7 _____

8 _____

Come to London!

1 *go shopping* _____

2 _____

3 _____

Come to Argentina!

9 _____

10 _____

11 _____

Grammar: Simple past of irregular verbs: questions

3 ★ Complete the conversation with the correct form of the verbs in parentheses.

Me: **1** *Did* you *have* (have) a good vacation?

Magali: Yes, we **2** _____ a great time.

Me: Where **3** _____ you _____ (go)?

Ernesto: We **4** _____ to six countries. France, Belgium, Italy, Germany, Switzerland, and Greece.

Me: What **5** _____ you _____ (do) at night?

Magali: We **6** _____ (not do) much. We biked all day, and we were very tired at night.

Me: Where **7** _____ you _____ (stay)?

Ernesto: We **8** _____ in hostels and camping grounds.

Me: **9** _____ you _____ (see) any interesting things?

Magali: I **10** _____ a lot of Ernesto's back. He was always in front of me!

Use your English: Talk about vacations

4 ★ Match the questions (1–10) with the answers (a–j).

1 Did you have a good vacation?
2 Where did you go?
3 When did you go?
4 What did you do?
5 What was the weather like?
6 How long did you stay there?
7 What was the food like?
8 How did you travel?
9 What did you buy?
10 Who did you go with?

a) We went to Greece.
b) It was beautiful. It was sunny every day.
c) We went by plane.
d) I went with my mom, my dad, and my brother.
e) Yes, I did. It was great.
f) It was great. I loved the Greek salads.
g) I bought souvenirs for my grandparents and my friends at school.
h) We went swimming every day.
i) We went for our summer vacation, in July.
j) We stayed there for two weeks.

Consolidation

5 Correct the conversation. There is one mistake in each sentence.

1 **A:** Did you <u>had</u> a good vacation?
   Did you have a good vacation?

2 **A:** Did you <u>went</u> on any tours?
   Did you go on any tours?

3 **B:** Not way! I hate tours.
   _____

4 **A:** Where you went?
   _____

5 **B:** We go to Chile.
   _____

6 **A:** Did you stayed in a hotel?
   _____

7 **B:** No. We did stay in a friend's house.
   _____

8 **A:** What the food was like?
   _____

9 **B:** Fantastic! I'm love Mexican food.
   _____

10 **A:** Hey! Wait a minutes. I thought you were in Chile!
   _____

Three days ago we saw the waterfalls.

Vocabulary: Landforms

1 ★ **Unscramble the letters to make landform words.**

1 tasco	_coast_	4 verir	_____	7 inoutman	_____
2 lihl	_____	5 anceo	_____	8 latwafler	_____
3 klae	_____	6 stofer	_____	9 sandli	_____
				10 ase	_____

Grammar: Simple past with *ago*

2 ★ **Read Luisa's diary and complete the table.**

> *August 31, 10* P.M.
>
> *I can't believe I go back to school tomorrow. Mario texted me at the end of June and asked me to stay with him and his family. School got out on July 20. I flew to Lima on August 10. Only two weeks ago, we were walking around San Isidro in Lima! Now he is 2343 miles away ☹. We said good-bye at the airport at 2* P.M. *today, and I landed at 8* P.M. *I don't want to think about Peru or Lima now. I'm really sad. And five minutes ago, my parents tried to make me feel happy—they cooked my favorite meal and put on my favorite DVD!*

Event	Date / Time	Ago
Mario texted Luisa . . .	**1** *at the end of June.*	two months ago.
Luisa got out of school . . .	on July 20.	**2**
Luisa flew to Lima . . .	on August 10.	**3**
They were in Lima . . .	**4**	two weeks ago.
They said good-bye . . .	at 2 P.M.	**5** _____ hours _____ .
Luisa landed at the airport . . .	at 8 P.M.	**6** _____ hours _____ .

3 ★★ **Write sentences using the simple past and *ago*. It is now 11 P.M. on August 17.**

1 He / eat / Mexican restaurant / days (8/13)

 He ate at a Mexican restaurant four days ago.

2 He / go / supermarket / hours (10 A.M.)

 _____

3 He / visit / museum / month (7/17)

 _____

4 He / go / the movies / hour (8 P.M.)

 _____

5 He / buy / a book from the bookstore / days (8/15)

 _____

6 He / ate / Greek food / days (8/12)

 _____

7 He / climb / the mountain / weeks (8/3)

 _____

8 He / watch / a soccer game / hours (5 P.M.)

 _____

9 He / borrow / a book from the library / week (8/10)

 _____

Consolidation

4 Look at the pictures of Bruno's and Luz's amazing lives. Then complete the sentences using a word from each box.

> • ~~across~~ • across • across • ~~along~~ • along
> • in • down • up

> • forest • lake • mountain • ~~ocean~~ • river
> • sea • ~~valley~~ • waterfall

Bruno's amazing life

1 Bruno sailed _across_ the _ocean_ five years ago.

2 Three years ago, Bruno walked _along_ a _valley_.

3 Bruno walked _____ a _____ six months ago.

4 Bruno swam _____ the _____ one week ago.

Luz's amazing life

5 Luz walked _____ a _____ four years ago.

6 Luz biked _____ a _____ three months ago.

7 Luz swam _____ a _____ two weeks ago.

8 Luz climbed _____ a _____ five days ago.

Extra challenge!

5 ★★★ Write the places from the box in the correct category.

> • Amazon • Guadalupe • Iguazu
> • Cuicocha • Mediterranean
> • Mt. Everest • Pacific

• Mountain: _____

• Lake: _____

• River: _____

• Sea: _____

• Ocean: _____

• Island: _____

• Waterfall: _____

A new kind of explorer

Before you read

1 Before you read, check the meaning of these words.

> **New words**
> • real • army • soldier
> • parachute • paraglider
> • to raise money for charity

> **Learning strategy: Skim to get the general idea**
> **Remember!** When you read a text for the first time, read it quickly—or "skim" it—to get a general idea of what it's about.

Read

2 ★ Read the article quickly and circle the correct endings for the sentences.

1 Paragraph 1 is about Bear's . . .
  a) family.
  b) job.
  c) life in general.

2 Paragraph 2 is about Bear's . . .
  a) adventures.
  b) likes and dislikes.
  c) money.

Bear Grylls

Bear Grylls's real name is Edward. His family called him Bear when he was just one day old, and now everyone calls him Bear.

He's a British mountain climber, an adventurer, a writer, and a TV personality. He lives with his wife and two children on a boat on the River Thames. He joined the army and was a soldier for three years, but had to leave because he had a serious accident in a parachute jump.

But the accident didn't stop Bear. In 1997, Bear climbed Ama Dablam, a mountain in the Himalayas—a very difficult mountain to climb. Then in 1998, Bear climbed to the top of Mt. Everest. And if that wasn't enough, in 2003, Bear sailed across the cold North Atlantic Ocean in an open boat. Even more amazing, in 2007, he flew over the Himalayas on a paraglider when it was −76°C (−105°F). In doing this, he raised $1 million for charity.

3 ★★ Answer the questions about the article in full sentences.

1 What is Bear's real name?

His real name is Edward.

2 Where does he live?

_____

3 Why did he leave the army?

_____

4 What did he do in 1997?

_____

5 Where did he sail in an open boat?

_____

6 How much money did he raise for charity in 2007?

_____

Listen

4 ★ 🎧 11 Listen to the conversation and complete the chart about Helen Thayer's life.

Helen Thayer's life	
Born (country)	1 *New Zealand*
Born (year)	2
Went to the North Pole in . . .	3
Age when she went to the North Pole	4
Went to the North Pole with her husband in . . .	5
Walked across the Gobi Desert with her husband in . . .	6
Husband's age when he walked across the Gobi Desert	7
Traveled up the	8 _____ River by boat.

Write

5 ★ Write about Helen Thayer's life in your notebook. Use your notes from Exercise 4 to help you.

Helen Thayer is an explorer from New Zealand. She was born in . . .

- 1988 / North Pole / 50
- 1992 / return / husband
- 1996 / walk / Sahara
- Amazon / 2000 / boat
- walk / Gobi / husband / 2001 / 74

Vocabulary: Short adjectives

1 ★ **Match the adjectives (1–10) with their opposites (a–j).**

1 big — a) heavy / dark
2 good b) hard
3 slow c) long / tall
4 easy d) small
5 light e) cold
6 hot f) bad
7 clean g) dirty
8 short h) far
9 near i) young / new
10 old j) fast

Grammar: Comparative and superlative of short adjectives

2 ★ **Complete the sentences with the correct form of the adjective in parentheses. Then write the names of the three people pictured below.**

Name	Age	Weight	Height
A _____	56	165	5' 8"
B _____	41	149	6' 2"
C _____	23	189	5' 1"

1 Jerry's the _oldest_ (old) person.
2 Steve's _____ (tall) than Jerry and Daniel.
3 Jerry's _____ (heavy) than one person.
4 Steve's _____ (old) than Daniel.
5 Jerry's _____ (short) than one person.
6 Daniel's the _____ (heavy) person.
7 Steve's _____ (young) than Jerry, but he isn't the _____ (young).
8 Steve isn't _____ (heavy) than Jerry or Daniel.
9 Daniel's the _____ (short) person.
10 Jerry isn't _____ (tall) than Steve, but he's _____ (tall) than Daniel.

3 ★★ **Look at the information about three places and write sentences using the words given.**

Winter (January) beach vacations in South America

	Pinamar Argentina	Punta del Diablo Uruguay	Trancoso Brazil
Temperature:	79˚F	75˚F	77˚F
Distance from capital:	249m	185m	769m
Price per week:	$1750	$500	$4000
Population:	20,000	600	6,000
Good for teens:	★★★	★★	★★★★

1 Trancoso / big / town / Punta del Diablo
Trancoso is a bigger town than Punta del Diablo.

2 Punta del Diablo / near to the capital / Trancoso
Punta del Diablo is nearer to the capital than Trancoso.

3 Pinamar / hot / Punta del Diablo
_____

4 Trancoso / far from capital / Pinamar
_____

5 Trancoso / good for teens / Punta del Diablo
_____

6 Punta del Diablo / cheap / town
_____

Consolidation

4 Circle the correct words.

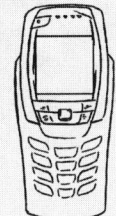

Cell phone monthly

New phones

Today, we're looking at three new cell phones on the market. The first is the XP121Z. It's a beautiful model. It's the **1** *light / lighter /* (*lightest*) of the three, at only 2.78 ounces. At $350, it isn't **2** *cheap / dirty / heavy*, and it's harder to use **3** *of / from / than* the other two models, but when you know what to do, it's great.

The SP25X is a nice phone. It's **4** *cheap / cheapest / cheaper* than the XP121Z, with a price of $150. It's a little **5** *heavier / bigger / taller*—3.5 ounces—but that's still nice and light. It's **6** *bad / easy / clean* to use. I like it.

The Z100 is a very **7** *old / older / oldest* phone, and it's very **8** *big / bigger / biggest*. It's the **9** *heavy / heaviest / heavier* of the three models, at 6 ounces. It isn't **10** *easy / light / cheap* to use. It's very **11** *hard / harder / hardest* to see the numbers. It has one good feature, the price! It's the **12** *hardest / lightest / cheapest*—$50!

We say: Buy the SP25X.

Extra challenge!

5 ★★★ Complete the quiz questions using the correct form of the adjectives from the box. Then try to answer the questions. Check your answers in the key below.

> • big • fast • high • ~~long~~ • old • tall

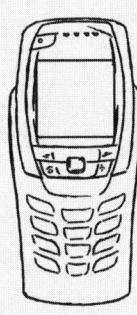

The BIG Quiz

1 Which is the longest river?
  a) Nile
  b) Amazon
  c) Mississippi

2 Which of these mountains is _____ than Mount McKinley?
  a) Kilimanjaro
  b) Aconcagua
  c) Pico Simón Bolívor

3 Which is _____ building in the U.S.?
  a) Sears Tower, Chicago
  b) Empire State building, New York
  c) U.S. Bank Tower, Los Angeles

4 Which is _____ car?
  a) McLaren F1
  b) Bugatti Veyron 16.4
  c) Porsche Carrera

5 Which ocean is _____ than the Atlantic?
  a) Indian
  b) Antarctic
  c) Pacific

6 Which is _____ university in Europe?
  a) University of Coimbra
  b) Oxford University
  c) University of Bologna

Vocabulary: Adjectives of quality

1 ★ **Circle the correct words.**

1 A: This is a (difficult) / exciting / important test.
   B: No, it isn't. It's easy.

2 A: Is that an interesting / famous / difficult book?
   B: No, it's boring.

3 This is a very difficult / talented / useful website. I get all my homework answers from it.

4 She's a boring / famous / beautiful actress. The whole world knows her name.

5 My son's very attractive / talented / difficult. He can sing, dance, paint, and play the guitar.

6 A: This is a beautiful / difficult / scary house.
   B: Thank you. I'm glad you like it.

7 Work hard. These exams are very attractive / talented / important.

2 ★★ **Complete the second sentences with adjectives from the box.**

> • attractive • boring • difficult • expensive
> • talented • useful

1 We don't understand this exercise. It's very _difficult_.

2 My parents never watch Hollywood movies. They think they're _____ .

3 I love Julia Roberts. Her hair looks really nice. She's a very _____ woman.

4 Betty can do lots of different things. She's really _____ .

5 Alex can do lots of things with his cell phone. He can't work without it. It's very _____ .

6 I really like that MP3 player, but it costs $275. That's very _____ .

Grammar: Comparative and superlative of long adjectives

3 ★ **Complete the conversations with the correct form of the adjectives given.**

1 difficult

Max: This homework is _difficult_.

Ben: Last week's homework was _more difficult_.

Max: Yes, that was the _most difficult_ ever!

2 famous

Jake: I like Manchester United because their players are very _____ .
        Wayne Rooney, Cristiano Ronaldo, . . . David Beckham played for them. He's the _____ player in the world.

Matthew: No, he isn't. Ronaldinho is _____ _____ than David Beckham.

3 exciting

Ellie: This is the _____ tennis match this year.

Laura: Do you think so? Last week's match was _____ than this one.

Ellie: Last week's match wasn't _____ . It was boring.

4 talented

Ryan: Do you think Jo is a _____ guitar player?

Mel: Well, she's OK. She's _____ _____ than I am!

Ryan: No, she isn't! You're the _____ _____ guitarist in the world!

5 useful

Nicola: I spend all my money on books. They're really _____ for studying.

Sara: Yes, but the Internet is _____ than books.

Nicola: Do you think so? What's the _____ _____ website you know for homework?

4 ★★ **Complete the e-mail with the correct form of the adjectives from the box.**

- attractive - difficult - exciting - famous
- interesting - talented - ~~useful~~

Mail

Hi Aunt Maria and Uncle Carlos,

Thank you for the birthday present. I love the online subscription to the encyclopedia! It's **1** *the most useful* resource I have! I always use it for my homework. School is good. This year is **2** _____ than last year—more exams, more homework, and more tests. But it's also **3** _____ _____ than last year because I'm taking more classes.

After school, I go to dance classes. The teacher is **4** _____ man I know. He can sing, dance, play the piano, and the guitar. He's great and he's **5** _____ than my music teacher at school! He has long, dark hair and dark eyes. **6** _____ news from here is that I was on TV last week! I'm now **7** _____ than Madonna at my school!

Thanks again for the very useful gift!

Love,
Amelia

Consolidation

5 **Write comparative sentences giving your own opinions using the cues.**

1 skiing / snowboarding (difficult)
   Snowboarding is more difficult than skiing.

2 skiing / snowboarding (exciting)
   _____
   _____

3 Winona Ryder / Cameron Diaz (famous)
   _____
   _____

4 Winona Ryder / Cameron Diaz (talented)
   _____
   _____

6 **Write superlative sentences giving your own opinions.**

1 exciting / sport
   I think the most exciting sport is (basketball).

2 difficult / sport
   _____

3 expensive / sport
   _____

4 talented / actress
   _____

Vocabulary: Clothes

1 ★ Write the names of the clothes in the correct places to find the word in the shaded boxes.

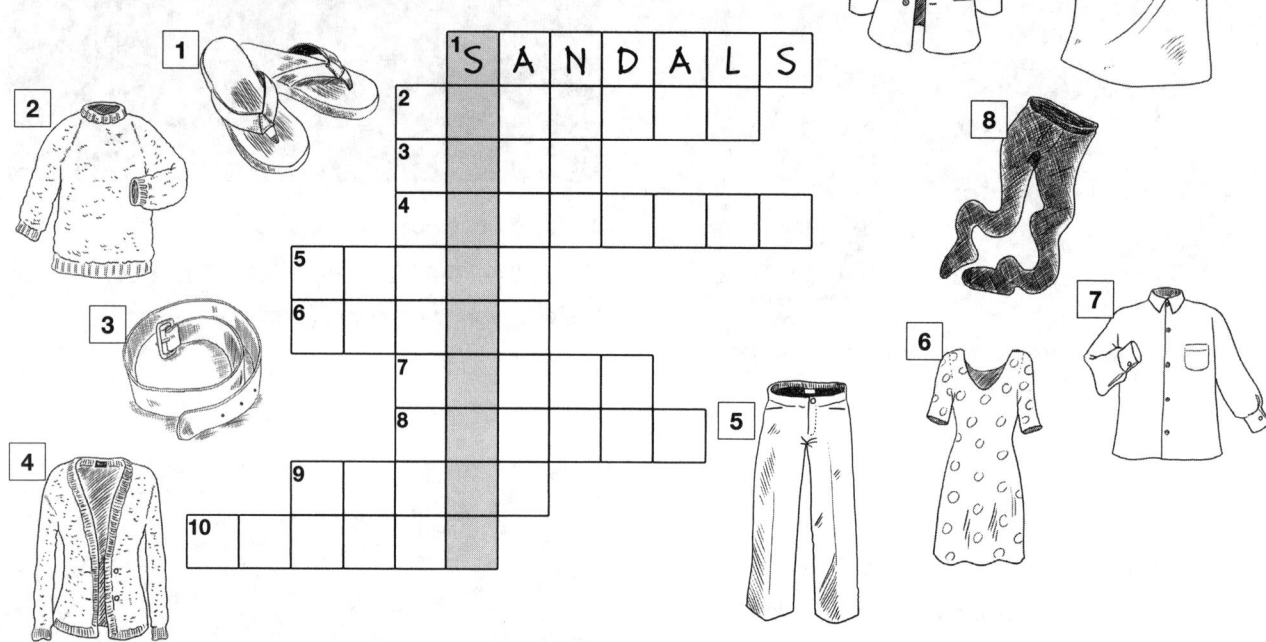

¹ S A N D A L S

Grammar: *Which* + indefinite pronoun: *one/ones*

2 ★ Rewrite the conversations using *one* or *ones* where possible.

1 A: I like that shirt.

   B: Which ~~shirt?~~

   Which one?

   A: That shirt over there.

   _____

   B: The green shirt?

   _____

   A: No, the blue shirt.

   _____

   B: Oh, that shirt.

   _____

2 A: Mom, where are my shoes?

   B: Which shoes? You have lots of shoes.

   _____

   A: My favorite old shoes.

   _____

   B: The black shoes?

   _____

   A: Yes.

   B: They're dirty. Wear your new shoes today.

   _____

Use your English:
Shopping for clothes
Too + adjective

3 ★ **Complete the sentences using *too* and adjectives from the box.**

• ~~big~~ • expensive • long • old • short • small

1 They're *too big* .
2 It's _____ .
3 It's _____ .
4 It's _____ .
5 They're _____ .
6 It's _____ .

4 ★ **Number the conversation in the correct order.**

Customer

a) Excuse me. Do you have a black jacket, please? `1`

b) This one is too small. Do you have a bigger one? ☐

c) Where are the fitting rooms? ☐

d) Great. I'll take it. `11`

e) This one's perfect. How much is it? ☐

f) Can I try this one on, please? ☐

Assistant

g) Of course. ☐

h) It's $75. ☐

i) They're over there. ☐

j) Yes, there are some black ones here. `2`

k) Yes, we do. Here you are. Try this. It's a bigger size, a 42. ☐

Consolidation

5 Complete the conversations with words from the box.

• fitting • much • on • one • pants • size • skirt • take • there • too • ~~try~~

1 A: Can I *try* these jeans _____ , please?
  B: Of course. The _____ rooms are over _____ .

2 A: I like the dark _____ , but not the light _____ . How _____ is it?
  B: It's $50.
  A: Great. I'll _____ it.

3 A: The boots are OK, but the _____ are _____ small.
  B: What _____ are you?

Values for living
Making friends

INTEGRATED
CONSOLIDATION
SKILLS

Before you read

1 Before you read, check the meaning of these words. Then read the blog posts each student wrote asking for advice.

New words
• accent • jealous • resent

2 My name is Samiya, and I'm from India. I've lived in the U.S. for four months now, and I'm going to Centerville High School. My problem is that I can't speak English very well. Some of the other students tease me about my English and about the clothes I wear. One new friend thinks my clothes are more attractive, and the other girls are jealous! I want to speak better English. And I want to make some more friends! Help!

1 My name is Gabriel, and I'm from Brazil. I've lived in the U.S. for one year now and am going to Richmond High School. I can speak good English, and I am a good student. My problem is that I am a better student than most of my friends. Some of them resent me for this. I work harder than they do, and I get higher grades. And here's another problem: the girls in my class think I am more attractive than some of my friends. I think they resent this, too! What can I do? I need some help!

3 My name is Luiz, and I'm from Colombia. I've lived in the U.S. for two years now, and I'm going to West High School. Other students sometimes laugh at my accent. And I'm not very good at playing soccer! My friends are helping me with my soccer skills. They think I'm playing better. But I don't know what to do about my accent. Help!

Read

2 ★ **Read the blogs quickly and match the people (1–3) with the statements (a–c).**

a) His/Her problem is that he/she has an accent. ☐

b) His/Her problem is that he/she cannot speak English very well. ☐

c) His/Her problem is that he/she is a better student and gets higher grades than his/her friends! ☐

3 ★★ **Read the blogs again. Are the sentences true (T) or false (F)?**

1 Luiz has a strong Indian accent. ☐ F

2 Gabriel's friends all get higher grades than he does. ☐

3 Samiya hasn't lived in the U.S. for a year yet. ☐

4 Luiz is becoming a better soccer player. ☐

5 Samiya wants to speak better Spanish. ☐

6 The girls in Gabriel's class think he is more attractive than his friends. ☐

Listen

> **Learning strategy: Listen for general meaning**
> **Remember!** The first time you listen, try to understand the general meaning of what is being said. Don't worry if you don't understand details.

4 ★ 🎧 12 **Listen to the conversation and circle the correct answers.**

1 Who is speaking at first?

a) Pedro

b) Victor

c) Pedro's dad

2 What is he/she talking about?

a) School life in New York City

b) Differences between life in New York City and Brazil

c) Problems at school

5 ★★ 🎧 12 **Listen again. What do the underlined words refer to?**

1 <u>It's</u> working now.   *Pedro's cell phone*

2 Pedro likes <u>it</u>.   _____

3 Pedro doesn't wear <u>one</u> to school in New York City.   _____

4 Pedro plays <u>this</u> at school.   _____

5 Pedro prefers <u>this</u> to soccer in New York City.   _____

6 Pedro's mom and dad do <u>this</u> at home.   _____

7 They don't have <u>these</u> for lunch at Pedro's school.   _____

6 ★ **Write an e-mail in your notebook from Samiya to an English-speaking friend in India. Imagine that she received good advice from bloggers! Use the ideas below and Exercise 6 on page 101 of the Student Book to help you.**

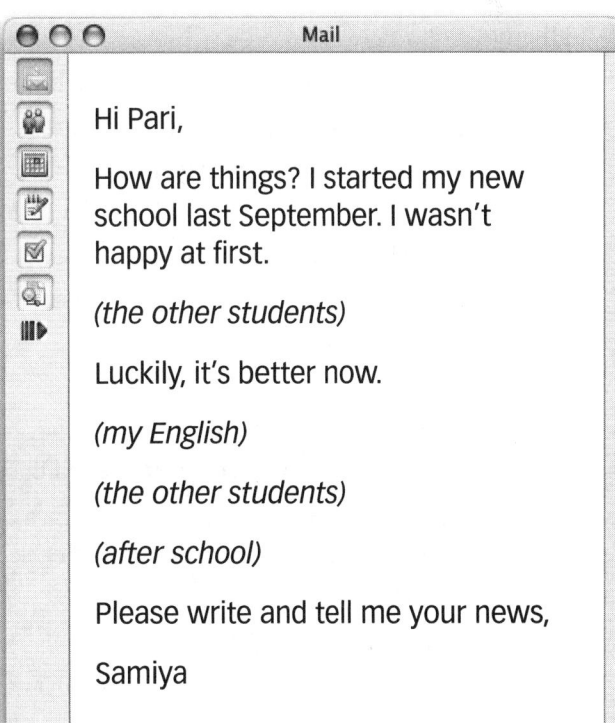

Hi Pari,

How are things? I started my new school last September. I wasn't happy at first.

(the other students)

Luckily, it's better now.

(my English)

(the other students)

(after school)

Please write and tell me your news,

Samiya

I'm going to record an album.

Grammar: *Be* + *going to* for future plans and intentions

1 ★ Look at the diary and complete the e-mail with the correct form of *be going to* and the verbs in parentheses.

Alan   **Bar**ry   **Ma**x

Sat Oct 1:	Concert: Newtown Youth Club
Sun Oct 2:	Concert: NOT ON
Mon Oct 3:	10 A.M. – Interview Seaside
	2–8 P.M. – Make CD
Tues Oct 4:	Me – Beantown: Meet DJs
	Band – wash the van

Mail

Hi guys,

Here are the plans for next week. On Saturday, you **1** *'re going to play* (play) a concert at Newtown Youth Club. On Sunday, you **2** _____ (not play) a concert. The High School doesn't want you. Monday **3** _____ (be) a busy day. The Seaside News **4** _____ _____ (interview) you in the morning, and in the afternoon, you **5** _____ _____ (make) your first CD! You **6** _____ (not have) much time in the studio, so don't be late. On Tuesday, I **7** _____ _____ (meet) some DJs in Beantown. You **8** _____ (wash) the van. It's disgusting!

Jason Briggs, Manager

2 ★★ Look at the next entries in the planner. Then complete the conversation with the correct form of *be going to* and appropriate verbs.

Wed Oct 5:	Alan: take photos for CD cover
	Barry: buy clothes for concert and cook dinner
	Max: start website
	Me: rest! Do nothing!
Thurs Oct 6:	NOTHING
Fri Oct 7:	Appear on TV show: "Future Stars"

Alan: What **1** *are* we *going to do* on Wednesday?

Jason: You **2** _____ busy. You **3** _____ photos for the CD cover. Max is the computer person, so he **4** _____ a website for the band. You can give him some photos for that. Barry can't use a computer and can't take photos.

Alan: So what **5** _____ he _____?

Jason: Don't worry. I've got two very important jobs for him. He **6** _____ clothes for your concerts and then he **7** _____ dinner.

Alan: **8** _____ you _____ anything?

Jason: No, I'm not. I **9** _____.

Alan: **10** _____ we _____ a concert on Thursday?

Jason: No, you aren't. You **11** _____ _____ anything on Thursday, but Friday's a very big day.

Alan: Why?

Jason: You **12** _____ on TV!

Alan: You're joking! TV! Well done, Jason.

Vocabulary: Types of music

3 ★ Unscramble the letters to make types of music.

1 My sister loves *pop* (opp) music.

2 I sometimes listen to _____ (pra) music.

3 My dad loves listening to _____ (zajz).

4 I bought a _____ (phi-pho) CD yesterday.

5 My friend's in a _____ (okrc) band.

6 _____ (alisclasc) music is very relaxing.

7 I don't like _____ (hontec) music.

8 I like _____ (niLat) music for dancing.

Consolidation

4 Complete the article with words from the box.

> • Are • aren't • aren't • be • ~~going~~ • going
> • is • Is • isn't • it • they're • to

Music Monthly

Big news!

Las Vegas band, "Panic! at the Disco" is **1** *going* to tour Brazil next year. In February, they're going **2** _____ release their new CD, and the first concert **3** _____ going to be in Rio in March. We also heard that **4** _____ going to film one concert for a DVD. **5** _____ they going to sell tickets on the Internet? No, they **6** _____ . You can buy tickets at the door.

There are lots of stories about the band on the Internet, so what is true? Well, don't worry, they **7** _____ going to break up! They're all good friends and love being in the band. And Ryan **8** _____ going to leave the band to go to college. Not this year! **9** _____ the music on the new CD going to be different? Yes, **10** _____ is. It's going to **11** _____ rock music, but with some jazz and Latin as well.

More news about the band next month. We're **12** _____ to interview the band in the U.S.

Extra challenge!

5 ★★★ Look at the pictures and correct what the people say they are going to do.

1 *Jerry isn't going to clean up the living room. He's going to watch TV* _____ .

2 Luke _____

_____ .

3 Carrie _____

_____ .

4 Sylvia _____

_____ .

Phrases

1 ★ Complete the conversations with phrases from the box.

- ~~Good luck!~~ • Let's start! • No problem! • Oh, man!

1 A: OK, boys, you're next. *Good luck!*
  B: Thanks.

2 A: Look at all those people. I can't do it! I can't!
  B: Come on, Timmy. _____

3 A: Look at Jimmy's guitar!
  B: _____ Now, what do we do?

4 A: Can we have a photo with you?
  B: Of course. _____

Grammar: Possessive pronouns
Question word: *Whose . . . ?*

2 ★ Circle the correct words.
1 A: *Who /* (*Whose*) book is this?
  B: It's *my / mine.*
  C: It's not *your / yours.* It's *José / José's.*

2 A: Is this *your / yours* bag?
  B: No, it isn't *my / mine.* I think it's *her / hers.*
  A: Whose?
  B: *Amelia / Amelia's.*

3 A: Is this Esteban and Mia's room?
  B: No, it's *our / ours. Their / Theirs* room is room 104.

3 ★★ Complete the second sentences so that they have the same meaning as the first.

1 This desk is my desk.
  This desk is *mine.*

2 Is this your CD?
  Is this CD _____?

3 Which is their house?
  Which house is _____?

4 This is our room, and that one is yours.
  That's _____ room, and this one's _____ .

5 Is this her computer?
  Is this computer _____?

6 This is his car.
  This car is _____ .

4 ★★ **Complete the sentences with the correct possessive pronoun or possessive 's.**

1 Don't eat that cake. It's _mine_ ! (It belongs to me.)

2 Look at this post. It's _Danni's_ . (It belongs to Danni.)

3 Dan's looking for his cell phone. Is this _____? (Does this belong to him?)

4 Don't read that e-mail. It's _____ . (It belongs to Cesar.)

5 Don't give that CD to Jade. It isn't _____ . (It doesn't belong to her.)

6 Ask Chris and Karen about this video game. It's _____ . (It belongs to them.)

7 Don't touch those sodas. They're _____ . (They belong to us.)

8 This isn't my DVD. Is it _____? (It belongs to Sergio.)

Vocabulary: Adverbs

5 ★ **Circle the correct words.**

1 Listen to the CD careful / (carefully) and do Exercise 4.

2 The weather is bad / badly today.

3 She played the CD loud / loudly.

4 Sit quiet / quietly. This is an exam.

5 Your computer's very slow / slowly. I think there's a problem.

6 Angie's very careful / carefully with money.

7 Julian walked out of the room quick / quickly.

8 This hotel's nice, but the room's noisy / noisily.

Consolidation

6 **Complete the conversation with words from the box.**

> • badly • Good • hers • Let's • man
> • mine • ours • q̶u̶i̶e̶t̶ • quietly • slowly
> • Theirs • yours

A: Can you be **1** _quiet_?

B: Why?

A: I'm trying to write a new song.

B: **2** _____ luck! Can we hear it?

A: "She's mine and I am **3** _____ .

I need her, oh so **4** _____ .

When she left me a year ago,

I sat alone so sadly."

Oh, **5** _____ . It's not very good, is it?

Do you have a song?

B: Yes, I do.

A: **6** _____ hear it, then.

B: "We walked **7** _____ through the park .

We talked **8** _____ in the dark .

She gave me love, I gave her flowers—

The most perfect love is the love that's

9 _____ ."

A: That's awful. Worse than **10** _____ .

B: No way!

C: Hey, guys, I have an idea.

A/B: What?

C: Let's sing some Beatles' songs. **11** _____ are much better than **12** _____ !

12c I want to see the video.

Grammar: *Want* + infinitive

1 ★ **Use the cues to write sentences about what the people want to do.**

1 I / go to a dance club

   I want to go to a dance club.

2 You / play tennis

   _____

3 Natalia / study French

   _____

4 Darren / buy a T-shirt

   _____

5 We / go to the movies

   _____

6 They / eat pizza

   _____

2 ★★ **Use the correct form of the words in parentheses.**

November 10

What 1 *do I want to do* (I / want / do) with my life? I 2 _____
(not / want / work) in an office, and I
3 _____
(not / want / worry) about money. I 4 _____
_____ (want / travel). What
5 _____
(my friend Sara / want / do)? She always studies
hard. She 6 _____
(want / go) to college. She 7 _____
_____ (not / want travel). Mark and Rob
8 _____
(want / start) a band; but Mark 9 _____
_____ (want / play) rock music,
and Rob 10 _____
(want / be) a rap singer!

Grammar: *Want* + object pronoun + infinitive

3 ★ **Rewrite the sentences with the words in parentheses in the correct place.**

1 They want to come. (us)

   They want us to come.

2 I want to come to my house. (you)

   _____

3 She wants to text her. (them)

   _____

4 Do you want to win the game? (me)

   _____

5 Does he want to sit here? (Cara)

   _____

6 We don't want to come. (Juan)

   _____

Use your English: Invite, accept, and refuse

4 ★ Complete the notes with words from the box.

- but • ~~like~~ • love • sorry
- sounds • want • What

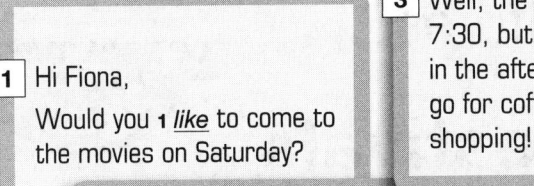

1 | Hi Fiona,
Would you **1** *like* to come to the movies on Saturday?

2 | Hi Molly,
Yes, that **2** _____ great.
☺ I'd **3** _____ to. **4** _____ time do you **5** _____ to meet?

3 | Well, the movie starts at 7:30, but we can meet in the afternoon. We can go for coffee or do some shopping!

4 | I'm **6** _____ ; I can't. ☹ I'd love to, **7** _____ I'm working in the afternoon. Let's meet at seven o'clock at the movies.

5 | OK, great. See you at seven.

Consolidation

5 Complete the story with sentences (a–g).

a) Do you want me to do these while you clean your room?

b) Do you want me to help?

c) My mom wants me to help her.

d) My mom wants me to wash these and then clean my room.

e) Sounds great!

f) Would you like me to drive you there?

g) ~~Would you like to go to the movies tonight?~~

Rafael: Hi. **1** *Would you like to go to the movies tonight?*

Matt: I'd like to, but there's a problem.
2 _____

Matt: **4** _____

Rafael: I have an idea. **5** _____

Matt: **6** _____

Rafael: Oh, Matt! **3** _____

Matt: Sure. Great!

Matt: All done.

Rafael: Oh no! The movie starts in 15 minutes!

Mom: **7** _____

Matt: Yes, please. Thanks, Mom!

Music festivals

Before you read

1 Before you read, check the meaning of these words.

New words
- Americana • annually • audience • attend • bluegrass
- blues • cabaret • circus • comedy • indie • middle-aged
- on average • punk • ska • spectators

1 You're invited to the biggest music festival in the U.K., the **Glastonbury Festival**. It's not just music. There's also dancing, comedy, theater, a circus, and cabaret. As many as 177,000 people attend the festival. The first festival was in 1971. Now it happens nearly every year in June. The festival includes some great new bands like The Killers and The Arctic Monkeys. One year, some people said that there were too many middle-aged people in the audience. Rock music isn't only for young people at Glastonbury.

2 Come to Rock al Parque in Bogotá, Colombia, for the biggest rock music festival in the world. One of many Festivals at the Park, it is the oldest and most famous one. It started in 1995 and is now held annually for three days. And the best thing is that it's free! The festival draws as many as 400,000 spectators. And there are more than 51 bands, on average, performing. Now, in addition to rock, it features punk, reggae, ska, and blues groups. You can watch two bands playing at the same time! It is an international festival with groups like Miranda! from Argentina, Los Bunkers from Chile, Haggard from Germany, and Mutemath from New Orleans.

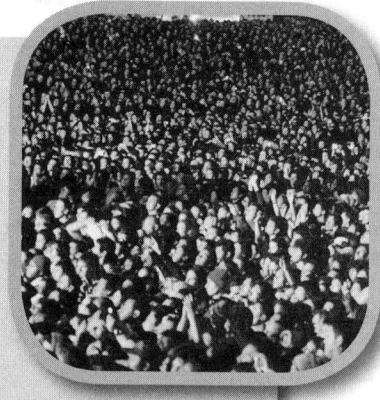

3 Mark your calendars for fall in Austin, Texas. That's when the three-day Austin City Limits Music Festival happens. With about 65,000 visitors a day, the festival is one of the best in the U.S. It began in 2002 as a two-day event, and now lasts for three. With about 130 bands on eight stages, you can hear rock, country, folk, indie, Americana, hip-hop, reggae, and bluegrass. If you're lucky, you'll hear big names like the American groups Pearl Jam and the Dave Matthews Band, Phoenix (from France), and maybe even Eek-A-Mouse, the Jamaican reggae artist.

Read

2 ★ Read the texts quickly and match the artists (1–3) to the festivals (a–c).

1 Eek-A-Mouse   a) Glastonbury

2 Miranda!   b) Austin City Limits

3 The Arctic Monkeys   c) Rock al Parque

3 ★★ Read about the three music festivals and write which festival each sentence describes.

1 You can listen to music and
   watch a circus or cabaret.   *Glastonbury*

2 This is the biggest rock
   festival in the world.   _____

3 This festival can have
   130 bands playing!   _____

4 This festival is the biggest
   in the U.K.   _____

5 This festival is free.   _____

6 This is the oldest and most
   famous of a group of festivals.   _____

4 ★★ Answer the questions about the three festivals.

1 When was the first Glastonbury festival?

_____

2 When was the first Rock al Parque festival?

_____

3 When did the first Austin City Limits Festival take
   place?

_____

4 At which festival can you hear rock, indie, and
   bluegrass?

_____

5 Which of the three festivals had the largest
   audience?

_____

6 Which festival takes place in South America?

_____

7 Which festival takes place in the fall?

_____

8 Which festival began as a two-day event?

_____

Listen

5 ★ 🎧 13 Listen to the conversation and answer the questions.

1 Where did Mia go? _____

2 Who did she go with? _____

3 Does her father like rock music? _____

4 What were the bands like? _____

5 What was the weather like? _____

6 What three things did Mia's father like?

_____

7 What is Mia going to do now? _____

Write

> **Writing tip: Organize your ideas**
> To organize your ideas and show the order of
> events in your writing, use sequence words such
> as *first*, *next*, *then*, and *finally*.
> **First,** they put on some fancy clothes.
> **Next,** they swim through freezing water.
> **Then** they run through the mud.
> **Finally,** they run back to where they started.

6 ★ Use the sequence words from the box to complete the sentences.

> • After (×3) • After that (×2) • First (×2)
> • then (×3)

1 *First* I put on my old clothes and _____ we
   had dinner. _____ dinner, we put our things
   in the car. _____ _____ , we drove to
   the festival.

2 _____ we arrived at the festival and _____
   we bought the tickets. _____ _____ , we
   watched some dancers. _____ watching
   the dancers, we went to see the bands.

3 _____ the bands finished, we went back to
   the car. Dad put on a CD and _____ we went
   home.

7 ★★ Write about your favorite festival in your notebook. Use the ideas in Exercise 1 to help you.

Grammar Bank

Welcome to the **Grammar Bank!**

- The **Grammar Bank** gives you extra practice of all the grammar points in each unit of the Student Book.

- At the beginning of each unit in the Grammar Bank, there is a *Grammar Summary* page with examples of all the grammar points from the unit and notes about grammar rules. You can use these to help you when you are doing an exercise, and as a check when you are reviewing.

- A set of *Grammar Practice* exercises follows each Grammar Summary. You can use these exercises as a follow-up to the exercises in the Workbook, or you can use them later to help you review.

- At the end of each unit is a *Consolidation* exercise, which covers all the grammar points from the unit.

1 Grammar Summary

The verb *be*

Affirmative
I'm **(am)** 13 years old.
You're **(are)** French.
He's **(is)** cool.
She's **(is)** my girlfriend.
It's **(is)** a big city.
We're **(are)** Spanish.
They're **(are)** 17.

Negative
I'm not **(am not)** American.
You **aren't (are not)** Greek.
He **isn't (is not)** the youth coordinator.
She **isn't (is not)** my sister.
It **isn't (is not)** the capital.
We **aren't (are not)** Italian.
They **aren't (are not)** 18.

Questions

Am I wrong?
Are you Spanish?
Is he Italian?
Is she your sister?
Is it the capital?
Are we in Spain?
Are you 13?
Are they from Quito?

Short answers

Affirmative	Negative
Yes, you **are**.	No, you **aren't**.
Yes, I **am**.	No, I'm **not**.
Yes, he **is**.	No, he **isn't**.
Yes, she **is**.	No, she **isn't**.
Yes, it **is**.	No, it **isn't**.
Yes, we (you) **are**.	No, we (you) **aren't**.
Yes, you **are**.	No, you **aren't**.
Yes, they **are**.	No, they **aren't**.

Subject pronouns and possessive adjectives

Singular subject pronouns	Singular possessive adjectives
I	my
you	your
he	his
she	her
it	its

Notes

The verb *be*
Form
- We usually use contractions in spoken English for affirmative and negative statements.
  He's 14. He isn't 15.
- We don't use contractions in affirmative short answers.
  Yes, I am. **NOT** ~~*Yes, I'm.*~~ ✗
- The contraction of *I am not* is *I'm not*.
  I'm not 14.
- In questions, the verb *be* comes before the subject.
  Are you the youth coordinator?
  Is he 15?

Common mistake
~~*You are the youth coordinator?*~~ ✗
Are you the youth coordinator? ✓

Subject pronouns
- *I* is always written with a capital letter.
- In English, the subject pronoun *you* is both singular and plural.

Possessive adjectives
- We use possessive adjectives before nouns to talk about something that belongs to someone.
  *Where's **my** cell phone?*

Grammar Practice

The verb *be*: singular

Affirmative

1 Complete the sentences with the correct contracted form of the verb *be* from the box.

• 'm • 'm • 're • 's • 's • 's

1 I *'m* Argentinian.

2 It _____ a cell phone.

3 I _____ the coordinator.

4 She _____ my sister.

5 You _____ 13 years old.

6 Your ring tone _____ cool.

Negative

2 Make the sentences negative. Write the long form and the short form.

1 I'm Russian.   5 I'm 17.

2 He's from France.   6 Anna's the coordinator.

3 You're my sister.   7 Paolo's Italian.

4 It's a cool club.   8 You're from Argentina.

Long form	**Short form**
1 *I am not Russian.*	*I'm not Russian.*
2 _____	_____
_____	_____
3 _____	_____
_____	_____
4 _____	_____
_____	_____
5 _____	_____
_____	_____
6 _____	_____
_____	_____
7 _____	_____
_____	_____
8 _____	_____
_____	_____

Questions

3 Write the questions for these answers.

1 *Where are you from?* _____
  I'm from the United States.

2 _____
  My name's Paolo.

3 _____
  No, I'm not American.

4 _____
  I'm 17.

5 _____
  No, you aren't in Class 2B.

6 _____
  That's Consuela.

7 _____
  Yes, she is my sister.

8 _____
  No, it isn't my cell phone.

Subject pronouns and possessive adjectives

4 Circle the correct words.

1 Who's *she* / *her*?

2 What's *she* / *her* name?

3 How old are *you* / *your*?

4 *It's* / *Its* ring tone is cool.

5 *I* / *My* am 15 years old.

6 Is this *you* / *your* book?

7 *He* / *His* sister's Marisa.

8 *It's* / *Its* a cell phone.

The verb *be*: plural

Affirmative

5 Write sentences using plural subject pronouns and the verb *be*.

1 Anna and Sam / 16

They're 16.

2 You and your brother / American

_____

3 My girlfriend and I / 17

_____

4 Julio, Jorgé, and I / Spanish

_____

5 Madrid and Seville / in Spain

_____

6 You, Sophie, and Mia / 15

_____

Negative

6 Correct the sentences using plural subject pronouns and the information in parentheses.

1 My friend and I are students. (teachers)

We aren't students. We're teachers.

2 You and Angie are 16. (15)

_____

_____

3 David and Victoria Beckham are American. (British)

_____

_____

4 My girlfriend and I are from São Paulo. (Rio de Janiero)

_____

_____

5 Bogotà and Cali are in Ecuador. (Colombia)

_____

_____

Questions

7 Write questions and answers using the cues.

1 A: you / American / ?

B: ✓

A: *Are you American?* _____

B: *Yes, we are.* _____

2 A: they / 14 / ?

B: ✗ / 13

A: *Are they 14?* _____

B: *No, they aren't. They're 13.* _____

3 A: we / in Canada / ?

B: ✗ / the U.S.

A: _____

B: _____

4 A: Mario and Sergio / Mexican / ?

B: ✓

A: _____

B: _____

5 A: Who / they / ?

B: Maria and Juanita

A: _____

B: _____

Consolidation

8 Complete the conversation with one word in each blank. Contractions are one word.

Lucas: Hello, Manuel.

Manuel: Hello, Lucas.

Lucas: This **1** *is* my sister. **2** ____ name **3** ____ Sophie.

Manuel: Nice to meet you, Sophie. Desi, this is Lucas and this is Sophie.

Desi: Hello. **4** _____ _____ Mexican?

Lucas: No, **5** _____ _____ . We're Brazilian.

Desi: **6** _____ _____ parents Brazilian?

Lucas: No, **7** _____ _____ . They're Colombian.

Desi: Where **8** _____ _____ from in Brazil?

Lucas: We're from Brasília. **9** _____ the capital of Brazil.

Desi: **10** _____ Brasília a big city?

Lucas: Yes, it is.

2 Grammar Summary

Indefinite article: *a/an*

It's **a** book.
It isn't **a** cell phone.
Is it **a** new computer?
It's **an** ID card.
It isn't **an** apple.
Is it **an** exciting book?

Regular nouns: plural

book	books
key	keys
diary	diaries
country	countries
watch	watches
class	classes

This, that, these, those

this book	**these** sneakers
that hat	**those** keys

Possessive *'s/s'*

my brother**'s** bag
Juan**'s** sister
my parent**s'** car
the boy**s'** bikes

Subject pronouns and possessive adjectives

Subject pronouns	Possessive adjectives
we	our
you	your
they	their

How much is . . ./How much are . . .

How much are	
the burgers?	They're $4.50.
How much is	
a can of soda?	It's $1.00.

Notes

Indefinite article: *a/an*

- We use *a / an* before a noun when we talk about one person or thing.
- We use *a* before a consonant sound.
- We use *an* before a vowel sound (a, e, i, o, u).
- The sound of the first letter of the noun after *a / an* is important:
  a <u>u</u>niversity /yuː . . . / (consonant sound)
  an <u>M</u>P3 player /em/ (vowel sound)

Regular nouns: plural

- To make most nouns plural, we add *-s*.

Spelling rules
- When a noun ends in a vowel + *-y*, we add *-s*.
- When a noun ends in a consonant + *-y*, the *-y* changes to *-i* and we add *-es*.
- When a noun ends in *-ch, -sh, -ss, -s* or *-x*, we add *-es*.

This, that, these, those

- We use *this* and *these* to talk about things or people that are near us.
- We use *that* and *those* for things or people that are not near us.

Possessive *'s/s'*

Usage
- We use *'s* and *s'* to talk about possession.

Form
- We use *'s* after a singular noun.
- We use *'* after the *-s* of a plural noun.

Common mistake
~~This is the bike of my friend.~~ ✗
This is my friend's bike. ✓

How much is . . ./ How much are . . .

- To ask the price of something, we use **how much are** for more than one thing and **how much is** for one item or for a total amount. To be polite, especially when we ask for the total, we can add *please* after the question or the answer.
  *How much is that altogether, **please**?*
  *It is $5.75, **please**.*

Grammar Practice

Indefinite article: *a/an*

1 **Complete the sentences.**

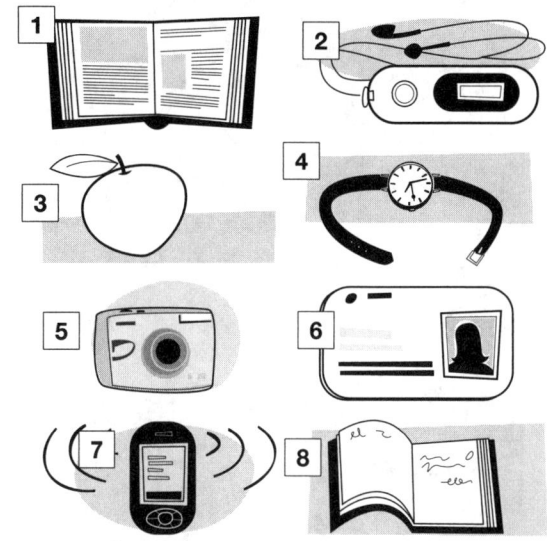

1 It's *a book* _____ .

2 It's _____ .

3 It's _____ .

4 It's _____ .

5 It's _____ .

6 It's _____ .

7 It's _____ .

8 It's _____ .

Regular nouns: plural

2 **Complete the chart with the correct singular or plural nouns.**

Singular nouns	Plural nouns
1 camera	*cameras*
2 notebook	
3	bikes
4 apple	
5	hats
6 key	
7	T-shirts
8 camera	
9 watch	

This, that, these, those

3 **Make the sentences plural.**

1 This isn't my pen.

These aren't my *pens* .

2 Is this your hat?

Are _____ your _____?

3 This is my notebook.

_____ are my _____ .

4 Is that Esteban's book?

Are _____ Esteban's _____ ?

5 This isn't Charlie's T-shirt.

_____ aren't Charlie's _____ .

6 Is this Mia's sandwich?

Are _____ Mia's _____?

7 Is this your key?

Are _____ your _____ ?

8 That is Angie's bag.

_____ are Angie's _____ .

Possessive *'s/s'*

4 **Circle the correct words.**

1 A: This is my sister.

B: Is this your *sisters'* /(*sister's*) bike?

2 A: These are my friends.

B: Are those your *friend's / friends'* bags?

3 A: This is Eduardo.

B: Is that *Eduardos' / Eduardo's* house?

4 A: Mr. Cuevo is my teacher.

B: Is that Mr. *Cuevos' / Cuevo's* pen?

5 A: These are my parents.

B: Is that your *parent's / parents'* car?

6 A: This is my band.

B: Are these your *band's / bands'* CDs?

7 A: This is Amelia.

B: Is that *Amelia's / Amelias'* bag?

Subject pronouns and possessive adjectives

5 Complete the text with the words in the box.

> • Our • our • our • our
> • Their • They • We • your

Hi! **1** _Our_ names are Danni and Emma.

2 _____ 're from Bradford in Yorkshire in the U.K., and this is **3** _____ website. It's all about

4 _____ favorite band, The Kaiser Chiefs.

This is a photo of the band. **5** _____ names are Nick, Simon, Nick, Andrew, and Ricky.

6 _____ 're from Leeds in Yorkshire.

7 _____ favorite song is _Ruby_.

What's **8** _____ favorite Kaiser Chiefs song?

E-mail and tell us NOW!

How much is . . ./How much are . . .

Menu

Burgers	$4.25
Chicken Salad	$3.75
Soda	$1.00
Bottled Water	$1.25

6 Look at the menu and write questions for the answers.

1 _How much is a can of soda?_

It's $1.00.

2 _____

They're $4.25 each.

3 _____

Altogether, that's $5.25, please.

Consolidation

7 Read the interview with Johnny Depp and circle the correct answers.

Johnny **1** _____ is from a big family. His **2** _____ name's Danny, and his **3** _____ names are Christie and Debbie. They're from Kentucky.

His **4** _____ name is Vanessa Paradis. She's French. She's a singer and **5** _____ actress.

Where's **6** _____ home? **7** _____ have more than one home! **8** _____ 're in Los Angeles, France, and the Bahamas.

What's **9** _____ favorite band? The Rolling Stones. He thinks **10** _____ music is great.

1	(a) Depp	b) Depp's	c) Depps'
2	a) brother	b) brother's	c) brothers'
3	a) sister	b) sister's	c) sisters'
4	a) girlfriend	b) girlfriends'	c) girlfriend's
5	a) a	b) an	c) the
6	a) your	b) their	c) our
7	a) Your	b) He	c) They
8	a) Their	b) It	c) They
9	a) his	b) our	c) your
10	a) our	b) your	c) their

There is/There isn't (There's no)

Affirmative
There's a book on the shelf.
There's an armchair here.

Negative
There isn't a book on the shelf.
(There's no book on the shelf.)
There isn't an armchair here.
(There's no armchair here.)

Questions

Is there a book in the bookcase?
Is there an armchair in the living room?

Short answers

Affirmative	Negative
Yes, there is.	No, there isn't.
Yes, there is.	No, there isn't.

Definite article: *the*

There's a book on my desk. **The** book is new.
There's a stove in **the** kitchen.

There are/There aren't + some/any with plural nouns

Affirmative
There are some books.
There are some CDs.

Negative
There aren't any books.
There aren't any DVDs.

Questions

Are there any chairs?
Are there any blue walls?

Short answers

Affirmative	Negative
Yes, there are.	No, there aren't.
Yes, there are.	No, there aren't.

Prepositions of place

The wastebasket is **under** the desk.
There is a pen **in** the drawer.
The computer is **on** the table.
The wardrobe is **next to** the door.
There is a window **behind** the sofa.
There is a table **in front of** the window.

Notes

There is/There are

Usage

- We use *there is (there's)* with singular people or things and *there are* with plurals.
  ***There's** a sofa in the living room.*
  ***There are** two armchairs in the living room.*

Form

- In questions, the verb *be* comes before the subject *(there)*.
  ***Is there** a book on the desk?*
  ***Are there** any CDs on the floor?*

Common mistake
~~*Is a chair in the room?*~~ ✗
Is there a chair in the room? ✓

some/any

- We usually use *some* in affirmative sentences.
- We usually use *any* in negative sentences and questions.

Common mistake
~~*Are there some CDs here?*~~ ✗
Are there any CDs here? ✓

Definite article: *the*

- We use *a / an* when we talk about something for the first time, and it is not clear which thing we mean.
  *There's **a** desk in my room.*
- We use *the* with a singular or plural noun when we know which thing we are talking about.
  *There's **a** desk in my room. **The** desk is big. There's a computer on **the** desk.*

Common mistake
~~*There's a sofa in a living room.*~~ ✗
There's a sofa in the living room. ✓

Prepositions of place

- We use prepositions of place to say where somebody or something is.

Grammar Practice

There is/There are

1 Look at the pictures. Correct the sentences.

1 There are three cabinets in the kitchen.

There aren't three cabinets in the kitchen.

There are two cabinets.

2 There are four chairs in the kitchen.

_____

_____

3 There are two refrigerators in the kitchen.

_____

_____

4 There are three armchairs in the living room.

_____

_____

5 There are two lamps in the living room.

_____

_____

6 There's one book in the bookcase.

_____

_____

7 There's a CD player in the living room.

_____

_____

2 Complete the questions and short answers about the pictures in Exercise 1.

1 *Is there* a stove in the kitchen?

Yes, there is.

2 _____ any sofas in the living room?

_____

3 _____ a CD player in the kitchen?

_____

4 _____ a dishwasher in the kitchen?

_____

5 _____ any chairs in the kitchen?

_____

6 _____ a desk in the living room?

_____

7 _____ books in the bookcase?

_____

8 _____ a window in the kitchen?

_____

Definite article: *the*

3 Complete the advertisement with *a*, *an*, or *the*.

City apartments

In every apartment, there's **1** _a_ kitchen, a bathroom, and a living room / bedroom. There's **2** _____ refrigerator, a sink, and a stove in **3** _____ kitchen. **4** _____ stove is new. There isn't **5** _____ dishwasher, but **6** _____ sink is very big.

In **7** _____ bathroom, there's **8** _____ bathtub and **9** _____ shower. In the living room, there's **10** _____ big window, and you can see downtown.

Some/any

4 **Six of the sentences are correct. Find the other five and correct them. Fill in the box.**

1 Are there some books here? [X]

Are there any books here?

2 There are some girls from the U.S. in our class. [✓]

3 Are there a refrigerator in the kitchen? []

4 There aren't any CDs on my desk. []

5 There is a stove next to the refrigerator. []

6 Is there some sofa in the living room? []

7 There isn't a bathtub in the bathroom. []

8 Is there any pens on the desk? []

9 There aren't some windows in the hall. []

10 Is there a teacher in the classroom? []

11 Are there some video games on the floor? []

12 There aren't any apples in my bag. []

Prepositions of place

5 **Circle the correct words.**

1 The pen is on the floor (under)/ in / on the desk.

2 This is a messy room. Why isn't this paper in / on / under the wastebasket?

3 The sofa is in front / behind / between of the window.

4 What's in / behind / on your desk?

5 There's a chair behind / in front / next to the desk.

Consolidation

6 **Read the conversation and complete it with words from the box.**

> • a • any • ~~are~~ • aren't • Is • on
> • some • the • there • there's • under

Miguel: Hi, Raul. How's my little brother?

Raul: I'm OK. Tell me about your new apartment.

Miguel: Well, it's OK. There **1** _are_ two bedrooms. I live with Marco. He's cool. He's from Buenos Aires.

Raul: **2** _____ there a TV?

Miguel: Yes, but it's small, and black and white.

Raul: Black and white! There aren't **3** _____ black and white TVs now!

Miguel: Well, it's very old! The living room's big. There are **4** _____ cabinets for our things, **5** _____ are two armchairs, and **6** _____ a big sofa.

Raul: Is **7** _____ sofa old?

Miguel: Oh, yes. It's all old. We're students, and we don't have much money.

Raul: Where are you now?

Miguel: I'm in my bedroom. There's **8** _____ desk in here. My computer's **9** _____ the desk. There's a wardrobe, there's a bed, and that's it. Oh, and there's a wastebasket **10** _____ the desk.

Raul: Sounds great!

Miguel: Yeah! Where are you? In your bedroom?

Raul: No, I'm in your room! Your CD player is great, but there **11** _____ any good CDs in here.

Miguel: You're joking! They're great CDs!

Raul: Sorry. They're not really my kind of music.

4 Grammar Summary

Have with I, you, we, they/Has with he, she, it

Affirmative
I **have** a sister.
You **have** a big house.
He **has** short hair.
She **has** curly hair.
It **has** a garage.
We **have** two cousins.
They **have** a daughter.

Negative
I **don't have** a brother.
You **don't have** an aunt.
He **doesn't have** blue eyes.
She **doesn't have** long hair.
It **doesn't have** a garden.
We **don't have** any children.
They **don't have** a son.

Questions

Do you **have** a brother?
Do I **have** an aunt?
Does he **have** a brother?
Does she **have** an aunt?
Does it **have** a garden?
Do you **have** any children?
Do they **have** a son?

Short answers

Affirmative	Negative
Yes, I **do**.	No, I **don't**.
Yes, you **do**.	No, you **don't**.
Yes, he **does**.	No, he **doesn't**.
Yes, she **does**.	No, she **doesn't**.
Yes, it **does**.	No, it **doesn't**.
Yes, we **do**.	No, we **don't**.
Yes, they **do**.	No, they **don't**.

Prepositions of time: *in, on*

My birthday is **in** August / May / July.
The school trip is **in** the summer / winter / spring / fall.
Our test is **on** Wednesday / Monday / Tuesday.
Christmas is **on** the 25th of December.

Notes

Have

Usage
- We use *have* to describe someone or to talk about possession.
  *She **has** brown hair.* (describing someone)
  *I **have** a dog.* (talking about possession)

Form
- We add *do(n't)* or *doesn't* to the verb *have* to make the negative.
  *I **don't** have a brother.*
  *He **doesn't** have brown hair.*
- In questions, *Do / Does* comes before the subject.
  ***Do you have** a brother?*
  ***Does he have** blue eyes?*
- We don't use *have* in short answers.
  A: Do you have a brother?
  B: Yes, I do. / No, I don't.
  NOT ~~Yes, I do have. / No, I don't have.~~

Common mistake
~~You have a brother?~~ ✗
Do you have a brother? ✓

Prepositions of time
- We use *in* with months and seasons.
  *My birthday is **in** the summer / **in** April.*
- We use *on* with days and dates.
  *The test is **on** Thursday / **on** May 30.*

Grammar Practice

Have with I, you, we, they

1 Complete the chart with affirmative or negative sentences.

Affirmative	Negative
1 I have a sister.	I don't have a sister.
2 My parents have a car.	
3	My friends don't have a new computer.
4 I have short, dark hair.	
5 We have a big TV.	
6	Kumar and Ilhan don't have my MP3 player.
7	They don't have ten cousins.
8	You don't have a dog.

2 Complete the text with the correct form of *have* (+ affirmative, – negative, or ? question).

Gabriel

March 12
My family

I have three comments from people about my family so . . .

1 (?) Do I *have* a big family?

Yes, **2** _____ . I **3** (+) _____ three brothers. I **4** (–) _____ a sister. My brothers and I are very happy.

We **5** (+) _____ great parents. My mother and father both **6** (+) _____ _____ two brothers. One of my mother's brothers, Uncle Sergio, is married, but my other three uncles **7** (–) _____ wives. Uncle Sergio and his wife **8** (+) _____ three daughters. They **9** (–) _____ any sons.

10 (?) _____ we _____ any animals?

11 Yes, _____ . I **12** (+) _____ a dog, and my cousins have a cat.

Tomorrow: My school.

4

Has with he, she, it

Name	Carmen	Name	Cesar
Eyes	green	Eyes	brown
Hair	long, straight, blond	Hair	short, dark
		Moustache	✓
		Beard	✗
Glasses	✓	Glasses	✗
Brothers	2	Brothers	0
Sisters	1	Sisters	2

3 Circle the correct words.

1 Carmen (has) / *doesn't have* green eyes.

2 Cesar *has* / *doesn't have* short, dark hair.

3 Carmen *has* / *doesn't have* two sisters.

4 Carmen *has* / *doesn't have* short hair.

5 Cesar *has* / *doesn't have* glasses.

6 Cesar *has* / *doesn't have* blond hair.

7 Cesar *has* / *doesn't have* blue eyes.

8 Carmen *has* / *doesn't have* glasses.

4 Correct the sentences about Cesar and Carmen.

1 Carmen has blue eyes.

   She doesn't have blue eyes. She has green eyes.

2 Cesar has a beard.

   _____

   _____ a moustache.

3 Cesar has a brother.

   _____

4 Carmen has three brothers.

   _____

5 Carmen has long, dark hair.

   _____

6 Cesar has three sisters.

   _____

Prepositions of time

5 Complete the text with *in* or *on* in each blank.

Special days in the U.K.

SPRING

Easter is **1** _____ the spring, but it can be **2** _____ March or April. Some schools have two Easter breaks. For Easter weekend, they have a holiday **3** _____ Friday and Monday, but they have a second Easter break **4** _____ March or April. This year, Easter is **5** _____ March 23, and our school's Easter break is from April 7–18.

Consolidation

6 Complete the conversation with the correct words from the box.

> • has • ~~have~~ • have • in • men • on
> • people • women

A: Hi, Hector.

B: Hi, Guido. What's new?

A: I **1** *have* a new girlfriend.

B: Hey, great. Tell me about her. What's her name?

A: Claudia. She **2** _____ long, blond hair and big, blue eyes.

B: Does she **3** _____ any brothers or sisters?

A: She's has three sisters. It's a big family. There are about 17 **4** _____ in her family.

B: What, 17 brothers and sisters?

A: No, no. Aunts, uncles, cousins . . . It's funny, all the **5** _____—her mother and aunts—are tall, and all the **6** _____—her father and uncles—are short.

B: How old is she?

A: She's 16. It's her birthday **7** _____ Monday.

B: Monday? So her birthday's **8** _____ March.

A: Yes. March 2.

Grammar Summary

Simple present with *I, you, we, they*

Affirmative
I **work** in a school.
You **work** in an office.
We **work** on a farm.
They **work** in a hospital.

Negative
I **don't work** in an office.
You **don't work** on a farm.
We **don't work** in a hospital.
They **don't work** in a school.

Questions

Do I **work** in a school?
Do you **work** on a farm?
Do we **work** in a hospital?
Do they **work** in a hospital?

Short answers

Affirmative	Negative
Yes, you **do**.	No, you **don't**.
Yes, I **do**.	No, I **don't**.
Yes, we **do**.	No, we **don't**.
Yes, they **do**.	No, they **don't**.

Simple present with *he, she, it*

Affirmative
He **works** in a school.
She **lives** in Brazil.
It **takes** three days.

Negative
He **doesn't work** in an office.
She **doesn't live** in Argentina.
It **doesn't take** a week.

Questions

Does he **live** in
Colombia?
Does she **live** in Ecuador?
Does it take **three** days
to get there?

Short answers

Affirmative	Negative
Yes, he **does**.	No, he **doesn't**.
Yes, she **does**.	No, she **doesn't**.
Yes, it **does**.	No, it **doesn't**.

Object pronouns: *me, you, him, her, it, us, them*

Subject pronoun	Object pronoun
I	me
you	you
he	him
she	her
it	it
we	us
they	them

Notes
Simple present
Usage
- We use the simple present to talk about things that are facts or are always true.

Form
- In affirmative sentences, *I, you, we,* and *they* all take the same form.
- In affirmative sentences, we add *-s* or *-es* to the verb for the third person singular *(he, she, it)*.
- We use *don't / doesn't* to make negatives.
- In negative sentences, there is no *-s* at the end of the verb in the third person singular.
- In questions, the word order is:
  do / does + subject + main verb + ?
- We use *do / does* in short answers. We do not repeat the main verb.
  Do you live in Italy?
  Yes, I do. / No, I don't.
  NOT ~~Yes, I live. / No, I don't live.~~

Common mistakes
~~He not like chips.~~ ✗
He doesn't like chips. ✓
~~Where you work?~~ ✗
Where do you work? ✓

Spelling rules
- We add *-es* to make third person singular affirmative forms *(he, she, it)* for verbs ending in:

-o	*go → goes, do → does*
-ch	*watch → watches*
-ss	*pass → passes*

- When a verb ends in a consonant + *-y*, we change the *-y* to *-i* and add *-es* in the third person singular form.
  study → studies
  BUT *play → plays* (vowel + *-y*, not consonant + *-y*)

Object pronouns
- We use object pronouns after verbs and prepositions.
  *Jake likes hamburgers. Jake likes **them**.*

Grammar Practice

Simple present with *I, you, we, they*

1 Complete the sentences with a verb in the simple present.

1 I *work* in an office.

2 My parents _____ in a big house in Lima.

3 My grandparents _____ in Brazil.

4 You _____ English, French, and Spanish.

5 We _____ to Brazil every year to see my grandparents.

6 At my school, the students _____ ten subjects.

7 My friends _____ on the school soccer team.

8 Jane's parents are doctors, and so they _____ in a hospital.

2 Complete the second sentences with the negative form of the verb.

1 I live in Cali.

I don't live in Bogotà.

2 I speak Spanish and English.

_____ French.

3 I live in an apartment.

_____ in a house.

4 We study English at school.

_____ French.

5 They work during the day.

_____ at night.

6 I go to the movies on Saturdays.

_____ to the movies on Sundays.

7 We want to work in a restaurant.

_____ in an office.

8 We play basketball at school.

_____ volleyball.

3 Use the cues to write questions for the answers.

Who am I?

Every week we ask you to read about a famous person and tell us who it is.

Telephone 800-555-1234, text 800-555-4321 or e-mail whoami@expressmags.com

1 **Q:** Where / you come from?

Where do you come from?

A: I come from Leytonstone in East London.

2 **Q:** you live / England now?

_____

A: No, I don't.

3 **Q:** Where / you live?

_____

A: In the U.S. In Los Angeles.

4 **Q:** What languages / you speak?

_____

A: I speak English and Spanish.

5 **Q:** Where / your parents live?

_____

A: They live in England. Near London.

6 **Q:** you live / apartment?

_____

A: No, I don't. I live in a house.

7 **Q:** you work / during the day?

_____

A: Yes, I do. I work in the afternoon and at night.

8 **Q:** Where / you work?

_____

A: I work outside.

9 **Q:** you play / soccer?

_____

A: Yes, I do. I play for LA Galaxy.

Simple present with *he, she, it*

4 Complete the text with the correct form of the verb in parentheses.

myfavoritestars.com

Kuno Becker is an actor. He 1 _is_ (be) from Mexico City. Now, he 2 _____ (live) in Los Angeles. He 3 _____ (act) in movies in Hollywood. He's an interesting person. He 4 _____ (speak) three languages: Spanish, English, and German. He 5 _____ (play) the violin very well.

6 _____ he _____ (like) his work? Yes, he 7 _____ . He 8 _____ (love) it and 9 _____ (not want) to do anything else!

Lots of people 10 _____ (know) Kuno because of the movie *Goal!* In the movie, Kuno is Santiago Muñez, a soccer player from Los Angeles. 11 _____ Kuno really _____ (play) soccer? No, he 12 _____ . Not really!

5 There are ten mistakes in the text. Find them and rewrite the text correctly in your notebook.

> **About me**
> My name is Carlos. My mother ⬭am⬭ from Leon, and my father is from Mexicali. He work in an office. My mother don't work. She is a stay-at-home mom. We do live in a small house near Mexico City. I goes to school there. I study English. My friend Miguel is study German. We doesn't study English at school. We study it at night at English Club. Miguel not speak English very much. I am want to work in a restaurant. Miguel don't. He wants to go on vacation.
>
> Carlos, there are lots of mistakes in your homework. Please write it again and give it to me on Thursday.

My name is Carlos. My mother is from Leon, and my father is from Mexicali . . .

6 Look at the information in the chart and write questions for the answers.

	Maria	**José**	**Angie**
live now	Seville	Quito	Caracas
from	Madrid	Santiago	Maracaibo
languages	Spanish, English	Spanish, French	Spanish, Portuguese

1 *Where does Maria live now?* _____
 In Seville.

2 _____
 From Santiago.

3 _____
 Spanish and English.

4 _____
 In Caracas.

5 _____
 Spanish and Portuguese.

6 _____
 From Madrid.

7 Complete the short answers.

1 Does your mother work here?

Yes, *she does* .

2 Do you work here?

Yes, _____ .

3 Does your sister study French?

No, _____ .

4 Do you live in a house?

Yes, _____ .

5 Do you and your friends like this restaurant?

Yes, _____ .

6 Do they work on Saturdays?

No, _____ .

7 Does your father live in Spain?

No, _____ .

8 Does your brother like chips?

Yes, _____ .

9 Do your parents work?

Yes, _____ .

10 Does your dog eat hamburgers?

No, _____ .

Object pronouns: *me, you, him, her, it, us, them*

8 Complete the text with the correct object pronouns.

What is the right thing to do?

Tonight, 7:00, Channel 2.

Tonight, Emilio Sanchez talks to people with problems.

- Carla doesn't like her job. "I hate **1** *it* . The people at work don't talk to **2** _____ , and I don't talk to **3** _____ . The manager, Mr. Soto, is friendly. I talk to **4** _____ every day, but it doesn't help. Please, Emilio, tell **5** _____ what to do."

- Jorgé and Ricardo don't want to go to school. "We don't like **6** _____ . The teachers are nice—we like **7** _____ —but the students don't talk to **8** _____ . They say we aren't cool. One girl, Sylvia, is nice. We like **9** _____ , but she's not in our class. Please, Emilio, tell **10** _____ what to do."

What do you think? What's the right thing to do? Emilio wants to hear from 11 _____ .

Consolidation

9 Find the mistakes and rewrite the sentences correctly.

1 Where you live?

Where do you live?

2 Amelia not like math.

_____

3 Where are my keys? I can't see it.

_____

4 I not want to live here.

_____

5 Eva want to work in a school.

_____

6 What your father does?

_____

Grammar Summary

Preposition of time: *at*/Simple present with fixed times

The store **opens at** nine o'clock.
The bank **closes at** 5 P.M.
The train **leaves at** 7 A.M.
The plane **arrives at** 5:45 P.M.

The class **starts at** 9:05 A.M.
The game **ends at** four forty-five.

Adverbs of frequency

I **always** get up at seven o'clock.
John **usually** has breakfast.
We **sometimes** go to the movies.
I **hardly ever** play video games.
We are **never** late for school.

Adverbial expressions of frequency

I take a shower   **once a day.**
I eat fruit   **twice a day.**
I brush my teeth   **three times a day.**

I go to the movies   **once a week.**
I play soccer   **twice a month.**
I visit my cousins   **three times a year.**

I watch TV   **every day.**
I hang out with my friends **every Saturday.**

Asking about frequency

How often do I / you / we / they help around the house?
How often does he / she eat fast food?
How often does it rain in Rio?
How often am I late?
How often are you / we / they tired?
How often is he / she / it correct?

Notes

Simple present with fixed times

- We use the simple present to talk about events or things that happen regularly.
  *Schools **start** at nine o'clock.*
  *The train to Boston **leaves** at 6 P.M.*

Common mistakes
~~What time schools start?~~ ✗
What time do schools start? ✓
~~The train leave at 6 P.M.~~ ✗
The train leaves at 6 P.M. ✓

Adverbs of frequency

- We use adverbs of frequency to describe how often someone does something or how often something happens.
- They come after the verb *be*.
  *I am **often** tired.*
  *He **is never** late.*
- They come before other verbs.
  *I **always go** to bed early.*
  *I **usually play** soccer on Saturdays.*
- *Sometimes* can come at the beginning or end of a sentence.
  ***Sometimes**, I watch TV.* ✓
  *I watch TV **sometimes**.* ✓

Adverbial expressions of frequency

- Adverbial phrases always come after the activity they describe.
  *I brush my teeth **three times a day**.*
  *I am late **three times a week**.*

Asking about frequency

- To ask about frequency using the verb *be*, we use:
  How often + verb to be (is / am / are) + subject + adjective
  ***How often are** you late?*
  ***How often am** I correct?*
- To ask about frequency using other verbs, we use:
  How often + do / does + subject + verb
  ***How often do** you eat fast food?*
  ***How often does** Julio exercise?*

Grammar Practice

6

Simple present with fixed times

1 Look at the information and circle the correct words in the e-mail.

Doors open: **6** P.M.
Concert:
7:15 P.M. – **10:35** P.M.

London 10:20 A.M.

Amsterdam 11:10 A.M.

Amsterdam **10:55** A.M.

Berlin **05:40** A.M.

NATIONAL BANK
Hours
09:30 A.M. – **03:30** P.M.

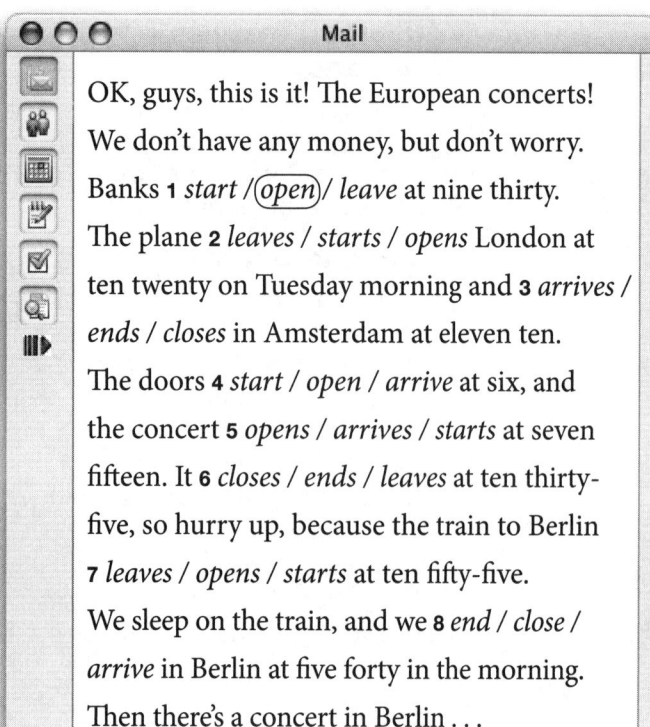

Mail

OK, guys, this is it! The European concerts!
We don't have any money, but don't worry.
Banks **1** *start /* open */ leave* at nine thirty.
The plane **2** *leaves / starts / opens* London at
ten twenty on Tuesday morning and **3** *arrives /
ends / closes* in Amsterdam at eleven ten.
The doors **4** *start / open / arrive* at six, and
the concert **5** *opens / arrives / starts* at seven
fifteen. It **6** *closes / ends / leaves* at ten thirty-
five, so hurry up, because the train to Berlin
7 *leaves / opens / starts* at ten fifty-five.
We sleep on the train, and we **8** *end / close /
arrive* in Berlin at five forty in the morning.
Then there's a concert in Berlin . . .

2 Complete the sentences. Use the simple present of the verbs in parentheses.

1 This store *opens* (open) at eight thirty.

2 Classes at our school _____ (start) at eight o'clock.

3 My last class _____ (end) at three thirty.

4 My father's office _____ (close) at 6 P.M.

5 Our soccer games always _____ (start) at 3 P.M. on Saturday.

6 Your train _____ (leave) at nine ten.

7 Trains from Boston _____ (arrive) here at three fifteen and six fifteen every day.

3 Complete the conversations.

1 A: Excuse me. What time *does* the store *open* ?

B: It opens at seven o'clock.

2 A: _____ the train from New York _____ at five o'clock?

B: No, it doesn't. It arrives at five forty.

3 A: When does the concert start?

B: It _____ at four thirty.

4 A: What time _____ banks _____ ?

B: I think they close at three.

5 A: Does the Brad Pitt movie end at nine o'clock?

B: No, it _____ . It _____ at nine thirty.

6 A: What time _____ this game _____ ?

B: It ends at five o'clock.

A: Oh, no! Only ten minutes left! Come on Yankees!

7 A: Do trains to Brooklyn leave at two o'clock?

B: Yes, they _____ .

8 A: _____ classes _____ at nine o'clock in your school?

B: Yes, they do. And they end at three thirty.

Adverbs of frequency

4 Put the words in the correct sentence order.

1 brush / in / my / I / the / always / teeth / morning.

I always brush my teeth in the morning.

2 you / tired / school? / at / often / Are

_____

3 your / always / eat / breakfast? / sister / Does

_____

4 parents / on / work / Sunday. / never / My / go / to

_____

5 sometimes / listen / music / bedroom. / my / to / I / in

_____

6 never / friends / at / night. / text / I / my

_____

5 Look at the information below about Esteban's week. Write sentences using the adverbs of frequency *usually, always, never, sometimes,* and *hardly ever.*

1 _He always plays video games in the evening._

2 _____

3 _____

4 _____

5 _____

6 _____

	Play video games at night	Read in bed	Take a shower in the morning	Have lunch at school	Be late for school	Watch TV in the morning
Monday	✓	✗	✓	✗	✓	✗
Tuesday	✓	✗	✓	✗	✗	✗
Wednesday	✓	✓	✓	✗	✗	✗
Thursday	✓	✗	✗	✗	✓	✗
Friday	✓	✗	✓	✗	✗	✓

Adverbial expressions of frequency

6 Complete the phrases.

1 Tuesday / Wednesday / Thursday

three days _a week_

2 May 15 / May 30 / June 15 / June 30 . . .

twice a _____

3 Mon / Tues / Wed / Thur / Fri / Sat / Sun

_____ day

4 morning / afternoon

_____ a day

5 10:00, 10:20, 10:40, 11:00. 11:20, 11:40 . . .

three times an _____

6 Monday / Monday / Monday / Monday

_____ a week

6

7 Put the words in the correct sentence order.

1 always / bed / go / I / early. / to
I always go to bed early.

2 a / We / on / year. / twice / go / vacation
_____

_____

3 goes / once / week. / Sam / swimming / a
_____

_____

4 get / a / We / times / homework / week. / three
_____

_____

5 shower / My / day. / sister / a / a / twice / takes
_____

_____

6 I / friends / five / an / text / hour. / my / times
_____

_____

Asking about frequency

8 Complete the questions.

1 How often *do you text* your friends?
I text my friends every day.

2 How often _____
to work?
My parents go to work five days a week.

3 How often _____ English?
I study English twice a week.

4 How often _____ with your family?
I hang out with my family three times a month.

5 How often _____
out? My brother goes out every Saturday.

6 How often _____ CDs?
My sister buys CDs once a month.

7 How often _____ TV?
I watch TV every night.

8 How often _____ to work?
Ben walks to work once or twice a month.

Consolidation

9 Complete the conversation with words from the box.

• always • arrive • arrives • ends • ever • every • once • start • starts • ~~usually~~

Meg: Hello, Sam. I don't 1 *usually* run into you in the morning.

Sam: No, I hardly 2 _____ go to school by bus. What time does the bus 3 _____?

Meg: At eight ten.

Sam: But it's eight ten now.

Meg: Don't worry. The bus is 4 _____ late.

Sam: Oh, no! I want to get to school at eight thirty today.

Meg: Why? Classes 5 _____ at nine.

Sam: I know, but I want to talk to Mr. Sanchez about the school soccer team. He always 6 _____ at eight thirty.

Meg: Do you play for the school team?

Sam: Yes, 7 _____ Wednesday.

Meg: Only on Wednesday?

Sam: Yes, only 8 _____ a week. Come and watch us on Wednesday.

Meg: I can't. I study Italian on Wednesday. My class 9 _____ at four thirty and 10 _____ at six o'clock.

Sam: Italian, eh? Say something in Italian.

Meg: *L'autobus è qui.* That means, "Here's the bus."

Grammar Summary

Can (present ability)/Adverb *(not) very well*

Affirmative
I / You / He / She / It / We / You / They **can swim**.

Negative
I / You / He / She / It / We / You / They **can't swim very well**.

Questions
Can I / you / he / she / it / we / you / they **run** fast?

Short answers

Affirmative
Yes, I / you / he / she / it / we / you / they **can**.

Negative
No, I / you / he / she / it / we / you / they **can't**.

Count and noncount nouns with *some* and *any*

Count nouns

Affirmative	Negative
There is **a** chicken.	There isn't **an** egg.
There are **two / three / some** bananas.	There aren't **any** grapes.

Questions

Is there **a** lemon?	Are there **any** onions?

Noncount nouns

Affirmative	Negative
There is **some** salt.	There isn't **any** pepper.

Questions
Is there **any** bread?

Imperatives

Affirmative		Negative	
Come here!	**Sit** down!	**Don't move!**	**Don't ask!**

Prepositions of place

The post office is **between** the bank and the drugstore.
The supermarket is **across from** the park.
The train station is **near** the coffee shop.
The parking lot is **behind** the movies.
The bookstore is **on the corner of** Park Street and Station Road.

Notes

Can (present ability)

Usage
• We use *can* + infinitive to talk about something we are able to do.

Form
• In negative sentences, we add *not* to *can (cannot)*. We use *can't* more often than *cannot*.
• In questions, the word order is: *Can* + subject + infinitive without *to* + ?

Common mistake
~~I can't to run five miles.~~ ✗
I can't run five miles. ✓

Count and noncount nouns

• Count nouns can be singular or plural. We can count them and we can use *a / an* or numbers with them.
• Noncount nouns:
  – are not usually plural
  – cannot be counted
  – don't have numbers or *a / an* with them
  – take the singular form of *be (is)*.

Some and *any*

• We usually use *some* with plural count and noncount nouns in affirmative sentences.
• We usually use *any* with count and noncount nouns in negative sentences and questions.

Imperatives

Usage
• We use the imperative to tell someone to do something.

Form
• We use the infinitive (without *to*) to make the imperative.
• We use *Don't* + infinitive (without *to*) to make negative imperatives.
• We use *please* at the beginning or end of an imperative to be more polite. ***Please** be quiet! / Be quiet, **please**!*

Prepositions of place
See Unit 3, page 105.

Grammar Practice

Can (present ability)/Adverb (not) very well

1 Complete the sentences using *can* or *can't* and the verbs in parentheses.

1 I *can cook* (cook).

2 My brother _____ (not dance) very well.

3 My parents _____ (not use) a computer.

4 Elena _____ (ride) a horse very well.

5 My friends and I _____ (play) basketball.

6 Ryan _____ (sing), but he _____ (not play) the guitar very well.

7 My little sister _____ (write) an e-mail, but she _____ (not send) it.

2 Complete the questions and short answers using the cues.

1 you / cook? ✓

   Can you cook?

   Yes, I can.

2 Maria / juggle? ✗

   _____

   _____

3 Rafael / sing? ✗

   _____

   _____

4 Pedro and Marisa / draw? ✓

   _____

   _____

5 you and your brother / swim? ✓

   _____

   _____

6 your mother / take good photographs? ✓

   _____

   _____

   _____

7 you and your friends / paint? ✗

   _____

   _____

3 Complete the sentences with words from the box.

> • can • can • can't • can't • not
> • very • well • well • you

How creative are you?

- **Can you play a musical instrument?**
  Yes, I 1 *can* , but not very 2 _____ .
- **Can you sing?**
  No, I 3 _____ .
- **What languages can 4 _____ speak?**
  I 5 _____ speak Spanish 6 _____ well and I can speak English, but 7_____ very 8 _____ . I 9 _____ speak any other languages.

Count and noncount nouns with *some* and *any*

4 Write the food items in the correct column.

> • bread • carrots • cheese • cookies • eggs
> • grapes • meat • onions • pasta • potatoes
> • salt • sugar

Count	Noncount
cookies	

5 Match sentence beginnings (1–8) to endings (a–h).

1 There is a
2 Are there
3 There isn't
4 Is there a
5 Is there
6 There aren't
7 There is
8 There are

a) any cookies?
b) any rice?
c) some grapes on the table.
d) refrigerator in the kitchen.
e) some food on the table.
f) any sugar.
g) any carrots here.
h) banana in your bag?

6 Look at the list and complete the sentences.

Food we have in the house

1 apples ✗
2 bananas ✗
3 bread ✓
4 butter ✗
5 oranges ✓
6 sugar ✓
7 potatoes ✗
8 rice ✗
9 salt ✗
10 chicken ✓

1 *There aren't any* apples.
2 _____ bananas.
3 _____ bread.
4 _____ butter.
5 _____ oranges.
6 _____ sugar.
7 _____ potatoes.
8 _____ rice.
9 _____ salt.
10 _____ chicken.

Imperatives

7 Write the verbs in parentheses in the correct form.

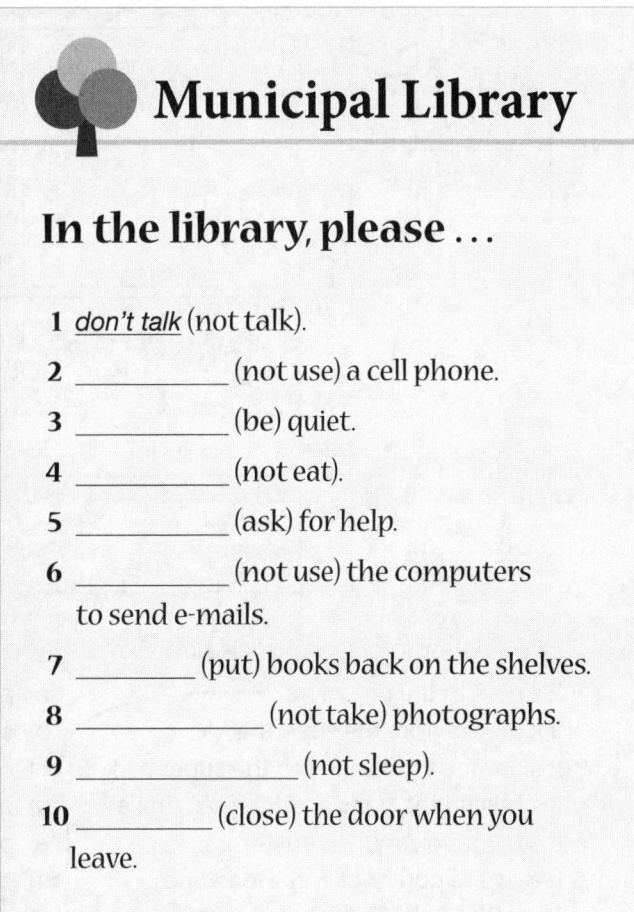

Municipal Library

In the library, please . . .

1 *don't talk* (not talk).
2 _____ (not use) a cell phone.
3 _____ (be) quiet.
4 _____ (not eat).
5 _____ (ask) for help.
6 _____ (not use) the computers to send e-mails.
7 _____ (put) books back on the shelves.
8 _____ (not take) photographs.
9 _____ (not sleep).
10 _____ (close) the door when you leave.

8 Complete the sentences with verbs from the box in the affirmative (+) or negative (–) form.

1 (–) *Don't watch* TV. (+) _____ your homework!

• be • buy • cook • do • go • look
• open • take • talk • ~~watch~~

2 (–) _____ out of the window.
(+) _____ your books.

3 (+) _____ quiet. (–) _____ during the exam.

4 It's eight fifty. (–) _____ a shower now. (+) _____ to school.

5 (–) _____ fast food.
(+) _____ dinner with me.

121

Prepositions of place

9 Look at the map and match the directions (1–8) to the places (a–h).

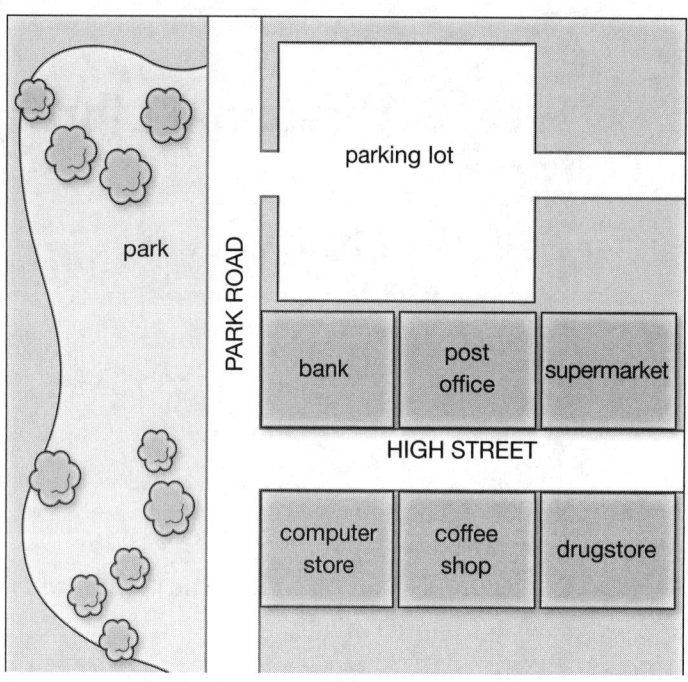

1 It's next to the drugstore.
2 It's across from the supermarket.
3 It's between the bank and the supermarket.
4 It's behind the bank and the post office.
5 It's across from the drugstore.
6 It's on the corner of Park Road and High Street, but it isn't next to the coffee shop.
7 It's on Park Road, but it isn't on High Street.
8 It's next to the coffee shop, but it isn't across from the supermarket.

a) post office
b) supermarket
c) computer store
d) park
e) parking lot
f) coffee shop
g) bank
h) drugstore

10 Look at the map and complete the directions.

1 A: Excuse me. Where's the bank, please?

B: It's *on the corner of* Park Road and High Street.

It's _____ _____the computer store and _____ _____ the post office.

A: Thank you very much.

2 A: Is there a coffee shop near here?

B: Yes, there is. It's _____ High Street

_____ the computer store and the drugstore.

A: Thank you.

3 A: Where's the parking lot?

B: It's _____ the bank and the post office.

Consolidation

11 Complete the conversation with words from the box.

> • any • are • Are • aren't
> • ~~Can~~ • Come • Don't • of
> • on • some • well

Sal: Hey, Raul. **1** *Can* you swim?

Raul: Yes, I can, but not very **2** _____ . Why?

Sal: There's a new swimming pool in town.

Raul: Really? Where?

Sal: It's in the sports center **3** _____ the corner **4** _____ River Road and Market Place. There's a swimming pool, and there are **5** _____ restaurants with healthy food!

Raul: Are there **6** _____ stores?

Sal: I don't know. **7** _____ with me and see.

Raul: Not today. There are some good TV shows on today.

Sal: **8** _____ watch TV. Come to town. We can have lunch. Some nice, healthy food.

Raul: I don't like healthy food. **9** _____ there any fast-food places there?

Sal: No, there **10** _____ , but there **11** _____ some good salad bars.

Raul: Well, OK. See you there in 30 minutes.

Present continuous

Affirmative

I**'m** (I **am**) **working**.
You**'re** (You **are**) **swimming**.
He**'s** (He **is**) / She**'s** (She **is**) **eating**.
It**'s**/The sun**'s** (It **is**/The sun **is**) **shining**.
We**'re** (We **are**) **dancing**.
They**'re** (They **are**) **sleeping**.

Negative

I**'m not using** my computer.
You **aren't studying**.
He/She **isn't going**.
It **isn't working**.
We **aren't cooking**.
They **aren't texting**.

Questions

Questions	Short answers	
	Affirmative	**Negative**
Am I **saying** it **right**?	Yes, you **are**.	No, you **aren't**.
Are you **writing**?	Yes, I **am**.	No, I**'m not**.
Is he **sleeping**?	Yes, he **is**.	No, he **isn't**.

Simple present and present continuous

I **usually work** on Fridays, but I**'m not working** today.
He **doesn't** often **eat** omelettes, but he**'s eating** one now.

Like, love, hate, prefer + -ing

I **like** swimming.
I **don't like** playing soccer.
He **hates** watching TV.
She **loves** reading.
I **prefer** swimming to jogging.
She **prefers** skiing to snowboarding.

Notes
Present continuous
Usage
- We use the present continuous to talk about things happening now.

Form
- In affirmative sentences, we use the verb *be (am / is / are)* + verb + *-ing*.
- For the first person singular negative, we add *not* after *'m / am*.
- For all other persons in negative sentences, we add *n't (not)* to the verb *be*.
- In questions, we put the verb *be* before the subject.

Common mistakes
~~*I playing soccer.*~~ ✗
I am playing soccer. ✓
~~*He doesn't playing soccer.*~~ ✗
He isn't playing soccer. ✓
~~*I amn't playing soccer.*~~ ✗
I'm not playing soccer. ✓
~~*You are playing soccer?*~~ ✗
Are you playing soccer? ✓

Spelling rules for *-ing* forms
- For most verbs, we add *-ing*.
  go → going
- When a verb ends in *-e*, we drop the *-e*, then add *-ing*.
  come → coming
- When a verb ends in one vowel + consonant, we double the final consonant.
  sit → sitting
- When a verb ends in *-ie*, the *-ie* changes to *-y*.
  lie → lying

Like, love, hate, prefer + -ing
- We use *like / love / hate / don't like* + verb + *-ing* to talk about likes and dislikes.
- We use *prefer* to compare two things.

Common mistakes
~~*I'm like playing video games.*~~ ✗
I like playing video games. ✓

8 Grammar Practice

Present continuous

1 Write the *-ing* forms of the verbs.

1 shine	swim	stay
shining [b]	*swimming* [b]	*staying* [a]
2 jog ___ ☐	speak ___ ☐	practice ___ ☐
3 take ___ ☐	talk ___ ☐	run ___ ☐
4 sit ___ ☐	make ___ ☐	do ___ ☐
5 write ___ ☐	win ___ ☐	walk ___ ☐
6 sleep ___ ☐	shop ___ ☐	dance ___ ☐

2 Now decide if the verbs in Exercise 1 are pattern a), b), or c).

a) add + *-ing*

b) drop *e*, add *-ing*

c) double the final letter, add *-ing*

3 Complete the sentences with the verbs in the correct present continuous form.

1 Magali *'s doing* (do) her homework. She *isn't watching* (not watch) TV.

2 My dad _____ (take) pictures.
He _____ (not work).

3 I _____ (not take) a shower.
I _____ (take) a bath.

4 Angie _____ (not play) video games. She _____ (read) a book.

5 We _____ (not cook) dinner.
We _____ (make) a cake.

6 Juan and Luz _____ (shop).
They _____ (not eat) out.

7 Marisa and Lucas _____ (not eat) pizza. They _____ (drink) soda.

4 Write questions and short answers using the cues.

1 your mom / go shopping? (✓)
Is your mom going shopping?
Yes, she is.

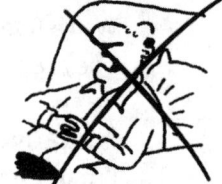

2 your father / sleep? (✗)

_____
_____

3 you / write / an e-mail? (✗)

_____
_____

4 your friends / take / pictures? (✓)

_____
_____
_____

5 your parents / cook? (✗)

_____
_____
_____

6 I / win / the game? (✗)

_____
_____

7 you and your friends / use / my computer? (✓)

_____
_____

5 Write the correct form of the verbs in parentheses.

Dear Consuela,

I'm in Verona, Italy. It's great. **1** I _'m staying_ (stay)
with my friend Alessandro. Right now,

I **2** _____ (sit) in a coffee shop.
The sun **3** _____ (shine), and we
4 _____ (drink) great Italian coffee.
Alessandro **5** _____ (text). His girlfriend
is on vacation, and he **6** _____ (write)
to her. I **7** _____ (have) a great time, but
I **8** _____ (not speak) a lot of
Italian—Alessandro and his parents speak very
good English. They **9** _____ (not sit)
with us right now. They **10** _____
(shop). Hope you're well. Have a great vacation.

Love,

Kate

La Lettera EUROPA

ITALIA   € 0.60

Consuela Silva
38 Ocean Ave.
Los Angeles, California
        90057
        U.S.

Simple present and present continuous

6 Circle the correct words.

1 I usually (play) / am playing tennis, but
   today I play / ('m playing) volleyball.

2 Tomás goes / 's going swimming every day,
   but he doesn't swim / isn't swimming now.

3 I don't often do / 'm not often doing
   gymnastics, and my friend doesn't often
   play / isn't often playing soccer.

4 We don't play / aren't playing volleyball
   now. We play / 're playing basketball.

5 "Do they play / Are they playing tennis?"
   "No, they don't / 're not. They sometimes
   play / are playing tennis, but today they
   play / 're playing soccer."

6 "Do you ever go / Are you ever going
   skiing in the winter?" "No, I don't / 'm
   not, but I sometimes go / am going
   snowboarding."

7 Mia hardly ever plays / is playing tennis,
   but she plays / 's playing very well now.

7 Use the words in the planner to write full sentences.

School trip
Thursday

1 8 A.M.: I – usually – go to school.
   Today – I – eat breakfast in the hotel.
   I usually go to school at eight o'clock. Today,
   I'm eating breakfast in the hotel.

2 11 A.M.: We – usually – have English.
   Today – we – visit a museum.

   _____

3 3 P.M.: José – usually – go home.
   Today – he – going to a barbecue.

   _____

Friday

4 11 A.M.: We – always – have a test.
   Today – we – walk in the park.

   _____

5 11 P.M.: I – usually – go to sleep.
   Today – I – talk to my new friends.

   _____

Like, love, hate, prefer + -ing

8 Complete the conversation using the words in parentheses.

Diego: **1** _Do you like hanging out_ (you / like / hang out) with your friends?

Luis: Yes, I do. I **2** _____ (love / go) to the mall, but my friends are on vacation.

Diego: **3** _____ (you / like / surf) the net?

Luis: No, I don't. I **4** _____ (not / like / use) computers.

Diego: What about sports? **5** _____ (you / like / play) tennis?

Luis: No, not tennis. I **6** _____ (like / go) skiing—but it's July now.

Diego: So what do your parents do in their free time?

Luis: What?

Diego: What **7** _____ _____ (your parents / like / do)?

Luis: Oh. My father **8** _____ (love / jog), and my mother **9** _____ (like / read).

Diego: You can go jogging with your father.

Luis: No way! I **10** _____ (hate / jog)!

Consolidation

9 Write sentences using the cues and the verb in parentheses.

1 **(watch)**
- like movies

  I _like watching movies_ .
- prefer to sports

  I _prefer watching movies to watching sports_ .
- usually watch two / three times a week

  I _usually watch movies two or three times a week_ .
- now—*Star Wars*

  Now I_'m watching_ Star Wars _____ .

2 **(write)**
- love e-mails

  My sister _____ .
- prefer to text

  She _____ .
- usually three a day

  She _____ .
- now—to her friend in Italy

  Now she _____ .

3 **(play)**
- love video games

  My friends and I _____ .
- prefer to sports

  We _____ .
- usually one hour a day

  We _____ .
- now—*Kong III*

  Now we _____ .

Grammar Summary

Simple past of *be*

Affirmative

Last night, I / he / she **was** tired.

I checked the mail, but it **was** late.

Yesterday, you / we / they **were** late.

Negative

I / He / She **wasn't (was not)** at home yesterday.

We expected a letter, but it **wasn't (was not)** there.

You / We / They **weren't (were not)** at school this morning.

Questions   Short answers

	Affirmative	Negative
Was I right?	Yes, you **were**.	No, you **weren't**.
Was he / she / it first?	Yes, he / she / it **was**.	No, he / she / it **wasn't**.
Were you busy?	Yes, I **was**.	No, I **wasn't**.
Were we / they ready?	Yes, we / they **were**.	No, we / they **weren't**.

Simple past of regular verbs

Affirmative

I / You / He / She / We / You / They **watched** the TV show.

It **ended** at 10:30.

Negative

I / You / He / She / We / You / They **didn't watch** the TV show.

It **didn't end** at ten o'clock.

Questions

Did I / you / he / she / we / you / they **watch** the TV show?

Did it **end** at 10:30?

Short answers

Affirmative

Yes, I / you / he / she / it / we / you / they **did**.

Negative

No, I / you / he / she / it / we / you / they **didn't**.

Prepositions of motion

We found the dog **across** the street.

First, he ran **along** the sidewalk.

Then he headed **down** to the park.

He went **up** the path.

He even walked **into** the grocery store!

He came **out of** the store very quickly.

He ran **past** all of the customers.

Notes
Simple past of *be*
Usage

- We use the simple past of the verb *be* to talk about the past.

Form

- There are two forms in the affirmative: *was* and *were*.
- We add *n't (not)* to *was* or *were* to make negatives.
- In questions, we put *was/were* before the subject.

Simple past of regular verbs
Usage

- We use the simple past to talk about actions and situations that started and ended in the past.

Form

- For the simple past affirmative of most regular verbs, we add *-ed*.
  look → looked; watch → watched
- We use the helping verb *didn't* + infinitive without *to* for negatives.
- In questions, the word order is *Did* + subject + infinitive without *to*.

Common mistakes

~~He didn't wanted to go.~~ ✗
He didn't want to go. ✓
~~Did he liked the movie?~~ ✗
Did he like the movie? ✓

Spelling rules

- When a verb ends in *-e*, we just add *-d*.
  arrive → arrived
- When a verb ends in one vowel + consonant, we double the final consonant.
  drop → dropped
- When a verb ends in a consonant + *-y*, the *-y* changes to *-i* and we add *-ed*.
  try → tried

Prepositions of motion

- We use prepositions of motion (*across, along, down, up, into, out of, past*) to tell where someone or something traveled or moved. Prepositions of motion are followed by an object, which is usually a noun or object pronoun.

Simple past of *be*

1 Circle the correct words.

1 I (was) / were late for school yesterday.

2 Julio *was* / *were* at the club on Saturday.

3 The soccer game *was* / *were* awful last night.

4 Kate and Emma *was* / *were* in my class last year.

5 You *was* / *were* tired this morning.

6 Sal *was* / *were* great in the concert last week.

7 My friends and I *was* / *were* on vacation in Rio last year.

8 Yesterday's homework *was* / *were* very difficult.

9 José's cousins *was* / *were* at the coffee shop last Saturday.

2 Complete the second sentence with a subject pronoun and the correct form of *was* or *were*.

1 Today, I'm on vacation.

Yesterday, *I was* at school.

2 Today it's sunny.

Last week, _____ sunny. It was cloudy.

3 Right now, we're in an English class.

At nine o'clock this morning, _____ in a science class.

4 This year, you're my friend.

Last year, you were at a different school and _____ my friend yet.

5 Today, Maria's at a concert.

Last night, _____ at a concert. She was at the movies.

6 Right now, I'm in my bedroom talking to you.

Last night, _____ in the living room.

7 Today, my parents are at home.

Yesterday, _____ at work.

8 My computer is very old.

In 2010, _____ old. It was very new.

3 Complete Angela's letter with *was / were* (+) or *wasn't / weren't* (–).

Dear Sophia,

I **1** (+) *was* in Washington, D.C. yesterday.

I **2** (–) _____ with my family.

It **3** (+) _____ on a school trip.

We **4** (+) _____ on the bus for two hours.

At 9:15, we **5** (+) _____ outside the White House. The President and his family **6** (–) _____ there! They **7** (+) _____ in Hawaii. At eleven thirty, I was at the Washington Monument. It **8** (+) _____ very exciting. You can ride the elevator to the top. After the Monument, we **9** (+) _____ hungry, but it **10** (–) _____ lunchtime. There was a long walk along the Potomac River first.

It **11** (+) _____ sunny, but it **12** (–) _____ very hot.

Love,

Angela

4 Complete the questions and answers about the school-trip schedule on page 129.

1 *Where were* the students at 8 A.M.?

They were on the bus.

2 Where was Angela at 9:15 A.M.?

_____ at the White House.

3 _____ the students at the Washington Monument?

They were at the Monument from 11 A.M. to 1 P.M.

4 _____ the students from 4 P.M. to 6 P.M.?

They were at the National Museum of Natural History.

5 _____ Angela at 7:30 P.M.?

She was on the bus.

School trip March 13

7:00	Bus leaves school
9:00	Bus arrives in Washington, D.C.
9:15–10:30	The White House
10:30–11:00	Walk to The Washington Monument
11:00–1:00	Washington Monument
1:00–2:00	Walk along Potomac River
2:00–3:00	Lunch by the National Mall
3:00–4:00	Boat ride along the Potomac
4:00–6:00	National Museum of Natural History
6:15	Bus leaves
8:15	Bus arrives at school

5 Look at the schedule above again and write questions using the cues. Then answer using short answers.

1 Angela / on the bus at 8 A.M.?

Was Molly on the bus at 8 A.M.?

Yes, she was.

2 the students / in Washington, D.C. at 8:30 A.M.?

_____

_____

_____

3 they / at the Washington Monument at 10 A.M.?

_____

_____

_____

4 Angela / by the National Mall at 2:30 P.M.?

_____

_____

_____

5 Angela / on a bus at 3 P.M.?

_____

_____

_____

Simple past of regular verbs

6 Complete the chart.

Base form	Past form
1 play	*played*
2 decide	
3	studied
4 like	
5 look	
6	walked
7 end	
8 cry	
9	watched
10 realize	

7 Complete the sentences with the simple past form of the verb.

1 My sister likes Metallica.

She *liked* the Spice Girls last year.

2 I play soccer now.

I _____ basketball when I was younger.

3 We walk to school every day.

We _____ to the mall on Saturday.

4 I'm watching a DVD now.

I _____ a different one last night.

5 My parents usually cook dinner for us.

Yesterday, my sister and I _____ dinner.

6 My brother is studying English this year.

He _____ French last year.

8 Complete the sentences with the correct simple past form of the verb in parentheses.

1 We *didn't walk* (not walk) to school this morning.

2 Darren _____ (decide) to go to the concert.

3 I _____ (study) hard for my exams last week.

4 My parents _____ (not want) to go to Spain on their vacation.

5 Nelly _____ (cry) when she watched the movie.

6 I _____ (not realize) you were here.

7 We _____ (finish) our exam at twelve thirty yesterday.

9 Read Alicia's diary and complete the questions.

> Friday
> We got out of school at three o'clock, and I walked into town with Tanya. We looked at CDs, and then I remembered it was Mom's birthday. I left and got home at five o'clock. I opened the door, and my aunt and uncle were there. They asked me about school and exams. Leo called me at about eight o'clock, and we talked for an hour. We decided to go to the movies tomorrow night. Great!

1 What time _did_ she _get_ out of school? At three o'clock.

2 Where _____ she _____ with Tanya? Into town.

3 What _____ they _____ at? CDs.

4 What _____ Alicia _____? That it was her mom's birthday.

5 What time _____ she _____ home? At five o'clock.

6 What _____ her aunt and uncle _____ her about? School and exams.

7 What time _____ Leo _____ ? At about eight o'clock.

8 Where _____ they _____ to go tomorrow night? To the movies.

10 Read the diary again and write questions and short answers about Alicia.

1 Alicia / get out of school at 3:30 P.M.?

Did Alicia get out of school at 3:30 P.M.?

No, she didn't.

2 Alicia / walk home with Tanya?

_____

_____

3 they / look at clothes?

_____

_____

4 Alicia / get home at 5 P.M.?

_____

_____

5 her aunt and uncle / ask her about pop music?

_____

6 Leo / text at about 8 P.M.?

_____

_____

Prepositions of motion

11 Complete the sentences with a preposition from the box.

> • across • along • down • up • into
> • out of • ~~past~~

Consolidation

12 Complete the text with the correct form of the verbs in parentheses.

The jogger ran **1** _past_ us. We watched him run **2** _____ the side of the river and then **3** _____ the hill—all the way to the top. Then later, we saw him run **4** _____ the hill and **5** _____ the bike path. We didn't see him again until we went **6** _____ the coffee shop to get some coffee. He was just coming **7** _____ the shop—and already starting to run again!

Lisa Star

Lisa Star **1** _was_ (be) born in 1985. When she was young, she **2** _____ (love) pop music and **3** _____ (watch) all the pop-music shows on TV. She **4** _____ (practice) singing every day. Lisa's parents **5** _____ (not realize) how good she was at singing.

She **6** _____ (work) hard at school and **7** _____ (pass) her exams. However, Lisa **8** _____ (decide) to quit school when she was 16 and **9** _____ (join) a band. Her parents **10** _____ (not be) very happy about this.

The band **11** _____ (play) their first concert at Lisa's school. Lisa's mom and dad were there, and they were so happy they **12** _____ (cry)!

10 Grammar Summary

Simple past of irregular verbs

Affirmative

I / You / He / She / We / You / They	**went** to Mexico City.
	bought a new book.
	ate dinner.
	took a shower.
It	**took** a long time.

Negative

I / You / He / She / We / You / They	**didn't go** to Mexico City.
	didn't buy a new book.
	didn't eat dinner.
	didn't take a shower.
It	**didn't take** a long time.

Questions

Did I / you / he / she / we / you / they	**go** to Mexico City?
	buy a new book?
	eat dinner?
	take a shower?
Did it	**take** a long time?

Short answers

Affirmative
Yes, I / you / he / she / it / we / you / they **did**.

Negative
No, I / you / he / she / it / we / you / they **didn't**.

By + means of transportation

To go / travel . . .
• **by** bus, car, taxi, train, plane, boat
• **on** foot

Simple past with *ago*

I finished school **two hours / three weeks / ten years ago**.
One year / two weeks / four months ago, I saw Brad Pitt.

Notes

Simple past of irregular verbs

Form
• Some verbs are irregular and do not form the simple past with *-ed*, for example:

have → had	do → did
go → went	know → knew
make → made	take → took
see → saw	get → got

• For negatives, we use *didn't* + infinitive without *to*.
• In questions, the word order is:
Did + subject + infinitive without *to* + ?

Common mistakes
~~I goed to work by bus.~~ ✗
I went to work by bus. ✓
~~I buyed a new cell phone.~~ ✗
I bought a new cell phone. ✓
~~He didn't went to school.~~ ✗
He didn't go to school. ✓
~~Did they met Manuel?~~ ✗
Did they meet Manuel? ✓

By + means of transportation
• To answer the question *How did you travel?*, we say:
I went / traveled **by** + (bus, car, etc.).
• But we say *on foot*:
I went to the beach **on foot**.

Common mistake
~~I went to the mall by foot.~~ ✗
I went to the mall on foot. ✓

Simple past with *ago*
• We use *ago* to say how many hours / days / weeks / years / etc. before now something happened.
(It's now 10 A.M. I woke up at 8 A.M.)
*I woke up **two hours ago**.*

Simple past of irregular verbs

1 Complete the chart with the past forms of the verbs. Not all the verbs are irregular.

Verb	Simple past form
1 get	*got*
2 go	
3 have	
4 leave	
5 make	
6 study	
7 take	
8 use	
9 work	
10 write	

2 Complete the second sentences with the past form of the verbs in bold.

1 I **go** to work by car.

Yesterday, I _went_ to work by bus.

2 You **buy** CDs every month.

Last month, you _____ three CDs.

3 I **take** a shower every morning.

This morning, I _____ a bath.

4 They usually **pay** $2 for a cup of coffee there.

Last week, they _____ $2.50.

5 We usually **leave** home at eight o'clock in the morning.

This morning, we _____ home at eight thirty.

6 My sister often **writes** e-mails to her friends.

On her school trip, she _____ three postcards and a letter.

7 My parents don't often **take** pictures at home.

They _____ lots of pictures on our last vacation.

8 Ernesto usually **does** his homework at night.

Today, he _____ his homework in the morning.

3 Write sentences using the cues and the correct form of the simple past.

1 I / not know / Miguel last year

I didn't know Miguel last year.

2 Yesterday / we / meet / our friends

_____

_____

3 You / not see / the new Spielberg movie / last night

_____

_____

4 My sister / get / an MP3 player for her birthday

_____

_____

5 My parents / eat / pizza every day on our last vacation

_____

_____

6 Nadia / buy / three books online

_____

_____

7 I / not speak / any English when I was in Brazil

_____

_____

4 Write short answers to these questions.

1 Did your friends have a party on Saturday? (✓)

Yes, they did.

2 Did you go out last night? (✗)

_____

3 Did your mother meet my mother yesterday? (✗)

_____

4 Did your brother take your CD? (✓)

_____

5 Did you and your friends make a cake? (✓)

_____

6 Did I do the wrong exercises for homework? (✗)

_____

5 Complete the questions and answers.

1 Where *did you go* (you / go) last night?

  I went to the movies .

2 What movie _____ (you / see)?

  I _____ the new Winona Ryder movie.

3 How much _____

  (pay / for) the ticket?

  I _____ $8.

4 _____ (you / meet)

  your friends?

  Yes, _____ .

5 How _____ (you all / get)

  to the movies?

  We _____ there by bus.

6 What _____ (you / eat) at

  the movies?

  I _____ popcorn and drank soda.

7 _____ (your brother /

  go) with you?

  No, _____ .

8 What _____ (he / do)?

  He _____ his homework.

Simple past with *ago*

6 Imagine it is the year 2069. Match the times (1–8) with the correct expressions using *ago* (a–h).

MARS HOLIDAY
TIME NOW: 5 P.M.
DATE: 10/25/2069

1 We left the U.S. on 10/23/2069.   *f*

2 Neil Armstrong walked on the Moon in 1969. ☐

3 We bought our ticket in July. ☐

4 We had dinner at 1 P.M. ☐

5 I woke up at 8 A.M. ☐

6 My friend on Earth e-mailed me at 4.45 P.M. ☐

7 They went to the Moon in 2059. ☐

8 The first Mars holiday was in March this year. ☐

a) three months ago

b) nine hours ago

c) seven months ago

d) 100 years ago

e) ten years ago

f) ~~two days ago~~

g) 15 minutes ago

h) four hours ago

7 Rewrite the sentences using the word in capital letters and *ago*.

1 I went to the movies at two o'clock this afternoon. It's now seven o'clock. **FIVE**

I went to the movies *five hours ago*   .

2 We had an exam on Monday. It's now Wednesday. **DAYS**

We had an exam _____ .

3 It's now May. My birthday was in January. **FOUR**

My birthday was _____ .

4 It's now ten thirty. My train left at ten twenty-five. **MINUTES**

My train left _____ .

5 We came back from our vacation on August 13 and it's now August 27. **TWO**

We came back from our vacation _____ .

6 It's now 8 P.M. and I finished my homework at 5 P.M. **HOURS**

I finished my homework _____ .

Consolidation

8 Complete the e-mail with the correct form of the verbs in parentheses.

Hi Ernesto,

Sorry I **1** *didn't write* (not write) to you yesterday. I was very busy. It was my mom's birthday.
I **2** _____ (make) a cake, and we **3** _____ (have) a party.

4 _____ (you / meet) Jack and Charlie last night? They **5** _____
(not write) to me, and I **6** _____ (not see) them today.

Talk to you later.

Lucas

P.S. **7** _____ (you / buy) the tickets for the concert?

Grammar Summary

Comparative and superlative of short adjectives

+ -er / -est
I'm **shorter** than you.
He's the **tallest** boy in the class.

+ -ier / -iest
This one is **heavier** than that one.
English is the **easiest** subject at school.

+ -r / -st
Elena is **nicer** than her sister.
The Flamingos are singing their **latest** song.

Double final consonant + -er / -est
Las Vegas is **hotter** than Miami.
São Paulo is the **biggest** city in South America.

Irregular adjectives
This is a **better** website than that one.
This is the **best** website I know.
The Moves are **worse** than Girls Alive.
The Moves are the **worst** band in the world!
Your house is **farther** from the school than my house.
Jack's house is the **farthest** from the school.

Comparative and superlative of long adjectives

This lesson is **more interesting** than yesterday's lesson.
I think Cameron Diaz is **more beautiful** than Angelina Jolie.

Do you think the Metropolitan is **the most important** museum in New York City?
Seth is **the most talented** musician in our class.

Which + indefinite pronouns one/ones

A: I like that shirt.
B: Which **one**? The blue **one** or the black **one**?

A: I want those jeans.
B: Which **ones**? The cheap **ones** or the expensive **ones**?

Notes
Comparative and superlative
Usage
- We use comparative adjectives to compare two people or things.
- We use superlative adjectives to compare a person or a thing with more than two people or things.

Form: comparatives
- When an adjective has one or two syllables, we add -er (than).
- For longer adjectives, we use more (than).

Form: superlatives
- When an adjective has one or two syllables, we add the + -est.
- For longer adjectives, we use the most.

Irregular forms
- There are three irregular comparative and superlative forms.
  good → better → the best
  bad → worse → the worst
  far → farther → the farthest

Spelling rules
- For adjectives ending in -e, we add -r or -st.
- For adjectives ending in -y, the -y changes to -i.
- For adjectives ending in one vowel + one consonant, we usually double the final consonant.

Common mistakes
I'm more faster than you. ✗
I'm faster than you. ✓
This is the goodest movie in the world. ✗
This is the best movie in the world. ✓
He's more intelligenter than I am. ✗
He's more intelligent than I am. ✓
We're older that you. ✗
We're older than you. ✓

Which + indefinite pronouns: one/ones
- We can replace a noun with the word one or ones. We use one with singular nouns and ones with plural nouns.

Grammar Practice

Comparative and superlative

1 Put the adjectives from the box in the correct column and write the comparative and superlative forms.

	+ -er / -est	y + -ier / -iest	+ -r / -st	Double final consonant + -er / -est	irregular
• bad • big • clever • easy • far • friendly • good • hot • heavy • late • near • nice • pretty • red • short • sunny • tall	short shorter the shortest	friendly friendlier the friendliest	nice nicer nicest	red redder the reddest	good better the best

2 Write comparative sentences using the cues.

1 I'm / tall / Luz

   I'm taller than Luz. _____

2 My car is / old / your car

   _____

3 Trains are / slow / planes

   _____

4 My town is / big / your town

   _____

5 German is / hard / English

   _____

6 My house is / far / from school / your house

   _____

   _____

3 Complete the sentences with the comparative form of the adjectives in parentheses.

1 This book is *more interesting than* (interesting) that one.

2 I don't think that Maria is _____ _____ (attractive) Danielle.

3 This DVD is _____ _____ (boring) the DVD we watched last week.

4 Motorcycles are _____ _____ (dangerous) cars.

5 Our English test yesterday was _____ _____ (difficult) the test last month.

6 Is Brad Pitt _____ _____ (famous) George Clooney?

4 Complete the sentences with the superlative form of the adjectives.

1 Tomás is tall, Juan is taller than Tomás, but Jorgé is *the tallest* boy in the class.

2 My house is big, your house is bigger than mine, but Julio's house is _____ .

3 This game is good, that one is better, but the new one at the mall is _____ .

4 Madrid was hot, Athens was hotter, but Cairo was _____ place I went to last year.

5 This band's first CD was bad, their second CD was worse than the first one, and their new one is _____ CD in the world!

6 My grandparents live far from us, my uncle lives farther away than them, but my aunt lives _____ _____ from us.

5 Write sentences using the cues and the superlative form of the adjectives.

1 What's / dangerous / animal in the world?

What's the most dangerous animal in the world?

2 What's / frightening / movie / playing now at the movies?

_____

_____

3 This is / important / day of my life.

_____

_____

4 Is German / difficult / subject in your school?

_____

_____

5 Marco is / talented / student in his class.

_____

_____

6 What's / exciting / video game you've played?

_____

_____

7 My dog's / beautiful / dog anywhere.

_____

_____

8 What's / useful / thing you learned at summer camp?

_____

_____

6 Look at the chart below. Complete the sentences about the video games.

1 *Halloween Night* / exciting

"Halloween Night" is the most exciting game.

2 *Tower Race* / interesting / *Pop Star Life*

"Tower Race" is more interesting than

"Pop Star Life."

3 *Soccer Team* / difficult

_____

4 *Halloween Night* / frightening

_____

5 *Halloween Night* / difficult / *Tower Race*

_____

6 *Tower Race* / exciting / *Soccer Team*

_____

7 *Halloween Night* / interesting

_____

8 *Pop Star Life* / easy / *Halloween Night*

_____

_____

9 *Tower Race* / boring / *Soccer Team*

_____

_____

10 *Pop Star Life* / boring

_____

_____

	Tower Race	Halloween Night	Soccer Team	Pop Star Life
Exciting?	✓✓	✓✓✓	✓	✓
Difficult?	✓	✓✓	✓✓✓✓	✓
Frightening?	✗	✓✓✓✓	✗	✗
Interesting?	✓✓	✓✓✓✓	✓✓✓	✓

7 Complete the conversation with the correct form of the adjectives from the box.

> • bad • beautiful • boring • ~~disgusting~~ • good
> • hard • intelligent • intelligent • interesting • lazy

Pablo: Hello, Juan. How was the school trip?

Juan: It was OK, but the hotel was the
1 _most disgusting_ hotel in the world!

Pablo: Who were you with?

Juan: There was José. He's very intelligent. The
2 _____ student in the
school. He's even **3** _____
than I am! Gabriel—he's the **4** _____
musician I know. He had a guitar and played
for us at night. It was great.

Pablo: Was Ernesto there?

Juan: Yes. He told jokes and stories all the time.
He told us awful stories at night! They were
5 _____ than your dad's stories!

Pablo: Was it an interesting trip?

Juan: Yes, it was. It was much **6** _____
than school. But it was **7** _____
than school, too. We had lots of work.
We walked all day and worked at night, but
the place was beautiful. It was the
8 _____ place anywhere.
But Cesar didn't like it. He said there was
nothing to do and it was the **9** _____
_____ place in the world. He
prefers big cities.

Which + indefinite pronouns one/ones

8 Complete the conversations with one word in each blank.

1 Francisco: Where's my hat?

   Mom: Which _one_ ?

   Francisco: The black _one_ .

2 Julio: Do you have my belt?

   Dad: _____ _____?

   Julio: The brown _____ .

3 Isabel: Where are my boots?

   Mom: _____ _____?

   Isabel: My new _____ .

4 Magali: Can I borrow some video games?

   Elena: _____ _____?

   Magali: The most exciting _____ you have.

Consolidation

9 Circle the correct words.

NEW: Exam help books

The **1** _more /(most)_ useful
books in the world!
2 _Cheaper / Cheapest_ than
other books!
3 _More / Most_ interesting
information than you can
find on the Internet!

EXAM
HELP BOOKS

ENGLISH
GRAMMAR

PLUS
Our new online help

The website is **4** _bigger / biggest_ than before! The
pages are easier to find, and the pictures are bigger
and better than the **5** _one / ones_ on the old site.

To help us write our books and website, we
have a team of the **6** _more / most_ talented
writers from some of the **7** _better / best_
universities in the country.

What people say about EXAM HELP BOOKS

• **8** _Better / Best_ than the Internet!

• I was the **9** _worse / worst_ student in my class
  and now I get **10** _higher / highest_ grades than
  all my friends!

We all need help, and there are lots of books for
sale. It's difficult to know which **11** _one / ones_ is
the **12** _better / best_. Now we know!

Be + going to for future plans and intentions

Affirmative

I**'m going to visit** my friends in Lima next week.
You / We / They **'re going to have** a party.
He / She**'s going to have** dinner at 7 P.M.
It**'s going to rain** tomorrow.

Negative

I**'m not going to visit** my friends in Lima next week.
You / We / They **aren't going to have** a party.
He / She **isn't going to have** dinner at 7 P.M.
It **isn't going to rain** tomorrow.

Questions	Short answers	
	Affirmative	Negative
Am I **going to see** you later?	Yes, you **are**.	No, you **aren't**.
Are you **going to have** lunch now?	Yes, I **am** / we **are**.	No, I**'m not** / we **aren't**.
Is he **going to text** you?	Yes, he **is**.	No, he **isn't**.

Possessive pronouns

Subject pronoun	Object pronoun	Possessive adjective	Possessive pronoun
I	me	my	mine
you	you	your	yours
he	him	his	his
she	her	her	hers
it	it	its	–
we	us	our	ours
they	them	their	theirs

Question word: *Whose . . . ?*

Whose sneakers are these? They're Gabriel**'s**.

Want + infinitive

I **want to go** out.
He **doesn't want to see** a movie.
Do they **want to play** soccer?

Want + object pronoun + infinitive

We **want you to help us**.
He **doesn't want his mother to go** with him.
Do you **want Tomás to call you**?

Notes

Be + going to for future plans and intentions

Usage

• We use the verb *be + going to + * infinitive to talk about future plans and intentions.

Form

• To make affirmatives, negatives, questions and short answers, we follow the same rules as for the verb *be* (see Unit 1).

Common mistakes

~~I going to go on vacation in June.~~ ✗
I'm going to go on vacation in June. ✓

Possessive pronouns

• We use these instead of *my / your /* etc. + noun.

Common mistakes

~~This is ours class.~~ ✗
This is ours. ✓
~~Where is mine hat?~~ ✗
Where is mine? ✓

Question word: *Whose . . . ?*

• We use *whose* to ask about possession.
• We use *'s* and *s'* to talk about possession.

Want + infinitive

• We can use a noun or a verb after *want*. We use a verb after *want* in the infinitive form.
• *Want* is not used in the continuous form.

Common mistake

~~I wanting to go out.~~ ✗
I want to go out. ✓

Want + object pronoun + infinitive

• The object always comes between *want* and *to +* infinitive.

Common mistake

~~I want him come with us.~~ ✗
I want him to come with us. ✓

Grammar Practice

Be + *going to* for future plans and intentions

1 Look at the to-do list and complete the sentences.

> Things to do this weekend:
>
> • Me – do homework
> • Julia – go shopping
> • Mom – work in the garden
> • Dad – wash the car
> • All – visit grandparents
> • Parents – have a party / buy a TV

1 I *'m going to do* my homework.
2 Julia _____ shopping.
3 Mom _____ in the garden.
4 My parents _____ a party.
5 We _____ my grandparents.
6 Dad _____ the car.
7 My parents _____ a TV.

2 Complete the sentences using *be going to* and the correct form of the verbs in parentheses.

1 I'm tired. I *'m not going to go* (not go) out tonight.
2 Oh, man! You _____

(not be) on the team next Saturday.
3 My brother _____

(not have) a birthday party next week.
4 Oh, man! Our teacher _____

(not work) here next year.
5 Great! We _____

(not have) an English test next week.
6 My friends _____

(not send) any texts tonight.
7 I _____

(not buy) their new CD.

3 Write questions and answers using the cues.

1 What / you / do / next weekend? (go to a party)
What are you going to do next weekend?
I'm going to go to a party.

2 What video games / you and your friends / play / tonight? (*FIFA Manager*)

_____

_____

3 What / your sister / buy / on Saturday?
(a new skirt)

_____

_____

4 What / your brother / study / in college? (History)

_____

_____

_____

5 Where / Isabel / go / on vacation? (Rio)

_____

_____

_____

6 Where / your friends / meet / after school?
(at the movies)

_____

_____

_____

7 When / the exam results / be ready? (next week)

_____

_____

_____

4 Look at the chart and complete the e-mail below with the correct form of the verbs.

Party—next Saturday	Me	Mom and Dad	Beatrice	Consuela
Make cake	✓	✗	✓	✗
Buy food and drinks	✗	✓	✗	✗
Clean the house after the party	✓	✗ – no help!	✗	✗
Invite friends	✓ – who?	✗	✓ – who?	✓ – who?
Take pictures	✗	✗	✗	✓
Be DJ	✗	✗	?	?

Hi Beatrice,

Good news. Mom and Dad say I can have a party! It's going to be on Saturday. I have some great plans. Mom and Dad **1** *are going to buy* the food and drinks, and you and I **2** _____ _____ a cake. Is that OK? Don't worry. I **3** _____ the house after the party! Mom and Dad **4** _____ help. It's my job!

You, Consuela, and I **5** _____ our friends to the party. We can do that tomorrow. Consuela **6** _____ pictures. She has a great camera. Now, the big question. Who **7** _____ the DJ? Not me. I want to dance!

What do you think?

Alfonso

Possessive pronouns

5 Complete the chart.

Possessive adjectives	Possessive pronouns
my	**1** *mine*
your	**2**
his	his
her	**3**
our	**4**
their	**5**

Question word: *Whose . . . ?*

6 Find and correct the mistakes.

Dino: Can I borrow ~~yours~~ book?
Victor: It's not mine. Who is it?
Dino: I don't know. Where's yours book?
Victor: In mine bag.
Dino: And where's your bag?
Victor: On the floor, next to your.
Dino: Are you sure? This bag's blue. Your is black.
Victor: My old bag was black. This one is new.

1 *your*	
2	
3	
4	
5	
6	
7	

141

Want + infinitive

7 Complete the questions using the cues and verbs from the box.

> • buy • ~~do~~ • eat • go • play • see
> • study • wear

1 What *do you want to do* (you / want) tonight?
2 Where _____
   _____
   (your parents / want) on vacation?
3 What _____
   _____
   (your brother / want) in college?
4 Which movie _____
   (you / want) Saturday night?
5 What game _____
   (they / want) this afternoon?
6 What _____
   _____
   (you / want) for dinner?
7 What _____
   _____
   (your sister / want) at the mall?
8 What _____
   (Manuel's girlfriend / want) to wear to the party?

Want + object pronoun + infinitive

8 Write the words in the correct sentence order.

1 want / do / dinner / to / you / for / What / us / cook / ?

   What do you want us to cook for dinner?

2 with / you / your / I / to / want / homework / help

   _____

   _____

3 want / your / me / at / Does / to / friend / computer / look / her / ?

   _____

   _____

4 on / the / want / be / school / team / Do / they / to / Magali / ?

   _____

   _____

5 doesn't / tonight / father / want / to / out / My / me / go

   _____

   _____

Consolidation

9 Circle the correct answers.

April 23

Dear Miss Hernandez,

Thank you for your letter about working at our Summer School Camp. We've had lots of letters, but **1** *yours* is one of the most interesting. We're **2** _____ have interviews with about ten people. The interviews **3** _____ going to take place in Phoenix on May 14th at 9 A.M. We want the interview **4** _____ a friendly, relaxed time, and so all the people coming for interviews are going **5** _____ in a hotel near **6** _____ office on the night before.
The interviews are going to last about an hour.
In the interview, we're going to **7** _____ you questions and, of course, we want **8** _____ to ask us questions, too.
Thank you again for **9** _____ letter.

Yours truly,

José Morales

Mr. J. Morales
Summer School Camp

1 a) you	b) your	c) yours
2 a) going	b) going to	c) go to
3 a) is	b) are	c) do
4 a) being	b) is	c) to be
5 a) stay	b) staying	c) to stay
6 a) our	b) ours	c) us
7 a) ask	b) asked	c) asking
8 a) you	b) your	c) yours
9 a) you	b) your	c) yours